PHILOSOPHY IN AMERICA
AN AMS REPRINT SERIES

LIVING RELIGIONS
AND A
WORLD FAITH

AMS PRESS
NEW YORK

LIVING RELIGIONS
AND A
WORLD FAITH

by

WILLIAM ERNEST
HOCKING

Alford Professor of Philosophy in
Harvard University

New York

THE MACMILLAN COMPANY

1940

Library of Congress Cataloging in Publication Data

Hocking, William Ernest, 1873-1966.
    Living religions and a world faith.

    (Philosophy in America series)
    Reprint of the 1940 ed. published by Macmillan,
New York, issued in series: Hibbert lectures, 1938.
    Includes index.
    1. Religions (Proposed, universal, etc.) 2. Religion.
3. Christianity and other religions. I. Title. II. Series:
Hibbert lectures (New York); 1938.
BL410.H6   1976   291   75-3187
ISBN 0-404-59189-2

Reprinted from an original copy in the collections
of the University of Virginia Library

From the edition of 1940, New York
First AMS edition published in 1976
Manufactured in the United States of America

AMS PRESS INC.
NEW YORK, N. Y. 10003

PREFACE

For a book put out in 1912 there was a concluding chapter which remained unpublished. The theme of the book was the meaning of God, so far as that meaning appears in human experience. The final chapters of the book as published had to do with "the prophetic consciousness" and with "God in history." The sort of "prophecy" there set forth was not the conventional myth of distant foreknowledge, but that assured control of the future, beginning with the immediate future, which may come from rapport with the deeper realities of event. I was attempting to present a realistic mysticism, one which turns its back on circumstance and the world's concerns only to find the Real, and thereby to renew energy and grit for the particular task, and to regain certitude in action, that detailed action whose integral sum is history.

The unpublished chapter dealt with the actual religions in their plural and historical character. It undertook to expound Christianity as the religion of "the prophetic consciousness." The germinal novelty of Jesus' teaching, it proposed, was not the doctrine of love in the accepted sense, but the doctrine of this sort of prophetic power: he expected of his disciples that faith "as a grain of mustard seed" which could "say to this mountain, be ye removed hence" and it would be removed—and he was himself, in this same sense, the prophet.

The time has come to rewrite a part of that chapter.

I am somewhat less unready than I then was to speak of the particular living religions. The circumstances of my life have kindly allowed me to visit the Near East and the Far East, to meet some of the great interpreters of religion there and here, and to see something of domestic religion in various parts of the world—the religion of villagers, farmers, artisans—not always in evidence in the books. It would require many lives to be sufficiently informed in this vast field. But one learns little by little two things: to sift out what is relevant to one's question, and to give conjecture its proper name and degree. With these two arts, one's inescapable ignorance loses part of its sting, and most of its power to mislead.

The invitation with which I have been honoured, to give a series of Hibbert Lectures, was accompanied by a definition of the task desired of me. In the series of these Lectures expositions had been given of many of the religions of the world, historic and living. There had been so far in the series no discussion of the rightful future relationships of the great religions, what attitudes they should hold to one another, and with what justification we might look forward to the prevalence of one of them as a world faith. This I was asked to undertake in four lectures. There was, I think, an added honour in the assumption that so much brevity could be achieved!

Such an invitation—especially in view of the unfinished work I have mentioned—had the force of a command, however little I could call myself ready for it. This task was not one of exposition: it was a task of judgment, and to some extent of recommendation—an exercise in practical reason. But its foundations are necessarily laid in one's philosophy, and in such intimations as one has of religious truth. Its conclusions will stand or fall with its metaphysics, or more strictly with its theology—which is accordingly the underlying issue of the book.

I am grateful to the Hibbert Trustees for the opportunity of bringing these discussions before the British public, and for the great pleasure, incident to delivering the Lectures, of closer association with colleagues in Cambridge and Oxford. I dare not begin to mention my large personal indebtedness, but I cannot forbear offering to Professor F. J. M. Stratton, of Gonville and Caius College, Cambridge, the tribute of peculiarly precious memories, and to Sir Michael Sadler, of Oxford, recognition of the support I found in his unique gifts of perception and friendship.

WILLIAM ERNEST HOCKING

MADISON, NEW HAMPSHIRE

July 14, 1939

ACKNOWLEDGMENTS

MANY of the specific illustrations given in these Lectures were the outcome of experiences during 1931–32, when as chairman of the "Commission of Appraisal" of the "Laymen's Inquiry" I went to India, China, and Japan in order to study the working of certain American Protestant missions. The Report of the Commission was published in the Fall of 1932 under the title, "Rethinking Missions." My special field of investigation was the indigenous religions, and I have to record the very great kindness of many an oriental saint and scholar in promoting these studies.

In the years immediately following the Report, it fell to my lot to give several series of lectures on this general theme, in the course of which many of the judgments expressed in the present book were ripened. I ought here to mention these lectureships: Alden Tuthill Lectures, University of Chicago; Hyde Lectures, Andover-Newton Theological School; Haskell Lectures, University of Chicago; Earl Lectures, Pacific School of Religion; Chancellor's Lectures, Queen's Theological College, Kingston, Ontario; Carew Lectures, Hartford Theological Seminary: Henry Martin Loud Lectures, Ann Arbor, Michigan. In view of the fact that the occasion was one of contemporary discussion, some of the Foundations on which I lectured waived their usual requirement of a published volume. The present book may, I trust, fulfil to some extent the omitted function.

Contributory to this book are two special studies

which I have been carrying on for a series of years in collaboration with colleagues in Harvard and abroad, one on the changes taking place in oriental religions, and one on the changing relations of religion and politics in different parts of the world. For the former of these I have had the use of a grant made in 1935 by the Milton Fund of Harvard University. For the latter, carried on in conjunction with Professors George Grafton Wilson and Sidney B. Fay, I have had the advantage of a grant from the Bureau of International Research of Harvard and Radcliffe. These studies are in progress.

Various authors and publishers have kindly permitted me to use excerpts from printed works:

> Harper and Brothers, Chapter iii of *Rethinking Missions* (here printed as Appendix ii).
>
> Rev. C. Burnell Olds and American Board of Commissioners for Foreign Missions, the article by Mr. Olds, "A Venture in Understanding," first printed in *Missionary Herald* (here printed as Appendix i).
>
> Willett, Clark and Company, quotation from *Is There a God?*
>
> Rev. S. M. Zwemer and Edwin E. Calverley, editors *The Moslem World*.

CONTENTS

LECTURE I
RELIGION AND RELIGIONS

THE SCANDAL OF PLURALITY

WHAT we have in the world is not religion, but religions. In its nature, religion is universal and one; yet everywhere it is local, partisan, plural. Followers of Moses, Confucius, Buddha, Jesus, Sankaracharya, Mohammed find themselves for the most part in separate camps. Is this a normal situation, or an historical accident which now, in the interest of world order, requires a remedy?

The mere existence of religious plurality is commonly felt to be a scandal. First of all, by the conscience of the religious man himself; for is not religion man's hold on what is eternal and true for all men, and therefore his deepest bond with his neighbour?

Then, by the philosopher, who usually professes to understand "religion," but not "a" religion, Professor John Dewey has recently written in behalf of "A Common Faith"; he recommends "religiousness" to mankind, but he regards as corruptions of natural piety all the specific supernatural apparatuses which serve the proprietary nostrums of organised religions. Philosophy usually feels that it has done a great deed if it has arrived so far as to recognise a God in the world; it has gained by the sheer use of reason a common ground with all the prophets; it is likely at this point to lose interest in their differences, and certainly in their peculiar historic establishments.

And now also by the statesman, who finds religious difference a weakness to the community, and who resolves, if there is to be any religion at all, to establish his own lines of unity and cleavage to the greater glory of the national state. The attitude of statesmen is not commonly regarded as weighty evidence in matters of religion. But I suggest that to-day it is of importance, partly because it is an external judgment, based on a distinct body of experience, and partly because it is taking religion seriously, even to the point of a determined campaign to eliminate it. The realistic politician no longer regards religion as a harmless indulgence of amiable sentiment; he sees that what men set up in their inner selves to reverence is a matter of the first magnitude for their worth as citizens, workers, and fighters.

In the Calcutta Conference of 1924, Motilal Nehru declared religion the chief barrier to the political independence of India; there could be no political unity until both Hindu and Moslem could detach themselves from their separative tenets. In Turkey until recently there was published from Stamboul a journal under the name of *Idjtihad*, an Arabic term for "discretion" as opposed to tradition. The editor, Dr. Djevdet Bey, was in the habit of printing on the back cover a set of principles: among them was this:

> The ostensible object of the religions is to develop among men the spirit of concord, of love and of compassion; it is preferable to abandon the remedy if, instead of curing, it aggravates and perpetuates the disease.

In this spirit, the new Turkey severs its official tie

with Islam, and with all religion. The newer Moslem
states of the Near East will not be likely to go so far.
Syria, preparing to legislate as a semi-independent
power, tries to define a position which will hold
religion and be free of the religions. A member of
the cabinet of 1938 writes me as follows:

> The state is neither irreligious nor does it belong to
> one sect at the expense of the others. It is not *laïque* in
> the sense that can be had from the attitude of Turkey.
> Its aim is, while belonging to all alike, to preserve in its
> people the spirit of religion—that religion which brings
> individuals nearer to what is ideal in character, dealings,
> social connections, worship.

These words illustrate a recent and rapidly spreading
tendency, defining a new alternative in the relations
of religion and state: unwilling to be partisan, and
unwilling to be religionless, the state will attempt to
define and use religion-in-general, without committing
itself to any religion-in-particular.* In taking this
direction, the statesman aligns himself with the philosopher in accepting religion while evading religions.

If there were an international statesmanship, we
might imagine that it would speak still more emphati-
cally in this vein. For how can there be an international
law or order or working league or federation of states
until there is an accepted level of moral understanding
among men to give vitality to its legal code? Religion
has its service to render to world order; but in its

---

* I should add that for certain parts of the proposed new legislation in
Syria, the law of inheritance, for example, the *Shari'a* or canon law of
Islam, was to be taken as a foundation, with special provision for other
communities.

divided state it contributes rather to the theory of impassable gulfs between East and West, between Nordic and Jew.

How did these divisions among religions arise? Will their origin throw any light upon their nature?

The existence of the great religions has an obvious historical explanation. Each one of them has gained its character and grown strong in a restricted region of the world, when intercourse with the rest of mankind was—not absent, but difficult.

Whether or not some of the ingredients of higher religion, such as the notion of immortality, had been disseminated from Egypt as a centre (as the Elliot Smith school of anthropology would have us believe) whatever elaboration religion received in India, Mesopotamia, Iran, China, must have been the work of sages and prophets indigenous to those lands. The great religions of Asia have grown up with the civilisations of the vast valleys and plateaus enclosed by their barriers of mountain and sea. Until the first century of our era, when Buddhist ideas made their dramatic entrance, China had to have a Chinese philosophy and religion, or none. And from then until, let us say, the sixteenth century when Europe began to be a telling factor in China, it had to have an Asiatic religion or none. Thus Confucianism and Hinduism bear the marks of strongly individualised local cultures; they fit those civilisations hand and glove, supporting them and giving them support. Buddhism, less local, is still a child of southern and eastern Asia. Christianity gained its characteristic

stamp within the limits of the Roman Empire. And
Islam, as a late birth, was able to grow strong in its
early years only because Arabia and the scene of its
first conquests were effectively insulated from a tur-
bulent and weakened Europe by distance and a difficult terrain. Nature prepares all strong growths in
secret: history allows no complete secrecy, but follows
the same model. The religions are many because the
world regions were many, while they were being
developed.

But if historical accident is the chief reason for
religious variety, history may undo it.

And history appears to be undoing it.

For the world was opened yesterday to the free
impact of civilisation on civilisation, and therewith of
religion on religion. And to-day, through the penetrating power of commerce and science, something
like a world culture begins to appear. With it, the
question is bound to arise whether a world religion is
not a necessary accompaniment of world culture, and
if so, what sort of religion it must be.

This is a wholly new question. It is radically different
in its motive and urgency from that of the religious
mission. The mission tries to make a particular religion
universal. The new interest is to escape particularity
and localism, finding in religions what is already
universal. The urgency behind it is not that of the
propagandist, but that of world citizenship. There is
a universal science; there should be universal law;
why may we not also expect a world faith?

The question is inescapable. It is the question which

detached common sense will always put to the scene of religious confusion. And it is a question which carries its own answer, an affirmative; if there is to be a world culture, and if there is to be any such thing as religion in the new order, there must be a world faith. In that sharp light, all one's localisms are seen to be local, and therefore unessential, relative, queer, afflicted with the staleness of ancient subjectivities, like a stuffy air which one can no longer endure to breathe once one has been outside in the freshness of a great morning. God is in his world, but Buddha, Jesus, Mohammed are in their little private closets, and we shall thank them, but never return to them. Such is the spirit of world citizenship at this moment.

The analogies to which this spirit appeals are, however, not wholly encouraging. Religion is in a different case from science. Science has no local marks. If space is the same everywhere, geometry must be the same. If physical nature is the same everywhere, physics and chemistry will be the same. Fauna and flora are not the same everywhere; but *life* is the same, everywhere on the planet; and the smell of a biological laboratory in Shanghai will put a visiting biologist from LaJolla or Woods Holl or Buenos Ayres immediately at his ease. But religion is heavily loaded with locality; it appears to be embedded in historical things such as custom, language, art, which are not universal. Nobody proposes that the world-culture should be characterised by custom-in-general; such an abstract distillate would be too tenuous to live, and too colourless to retain its interest. Is religion perhaps more like custom than it is like science?

Or consider the analogy of law. Law has its universal elements. There is such a thing as justice-in-general. The good judge and the bad judge have much the same traits in all ages and places; hence the ancient stories, such as that of the judgment of Solomon, never lose their point. The law of jettison valid in ancient Rhodes remains valid in any port of the modern world.* Nevertheless, law becomes international with great difficulty and hesitation. No code of justice-in-general can offer itself to replace the codes growing out of regional usage. Why is this?

Partly because justice *has to exist*; it cannot live as an idea alone, but must appear as operating in human decisions, in "cases" at law. It must present itself as a working factor in social life. And partly because the idea of justice *has to grow*, by way of this experience. Every new case has its points of difference from all previous cases; it cannot be decided by mere imitation or analogy; it adds its own item to what, in particular, justice means. Thus the cases develop the idea; and the idea guides the new cases, until through long experience mankind is clear what the essence of justice is; from that point, if it were reached, all legal decisions could be deductions from established principle; until that time, law must have its local history.

If religion is like law—and it is very like—it would seem that religion, too, must be an existent fact, not merely a rational idea, a fact working and embedded

* George Grafton Wilson.

in human practices, and growing with them toward clarity. It would be a long-continued social effort, guided indeed by some unfailing source of light, but having the character of an age-long prayer for rationality on the part of modes of behaviour and thought which are at any time only partly rational.

Perhaps the best analogy is that of language. For here the plea for a world language as a part of world culture seems fully as plausible as that for a world faith. And the obstacles to meeting this plea seem peculiarly instructive. There exist universal languages (unfortunately, they too are plural); but they do not mount saddle for any galloping triumph. They seem anemic, lacking in grit, deficient in the angular ugliness in which character and expressive qualities lurk.

There is a dilemma in the notion of a world-speech. It must be an actual speech, ergo irrational; it must be rational, ergo non-actual. Conclusion: there can be no world speech.

The strong trend which persists, to establish a common speech among men, takes the alternative form of promoting some one of the existing languages to that place. In this rivalry, each of the greater languages regards itself as the most natural candidate; for each group its language is already universal—or rather, it is simply language *per se*, the pure essence of communication. It is only to one who had travelled beyond France that the French language becomes "a" language among many, and so a relative thing rather than speech-absolute. And even so, he continues to feel that it possesses a peculiar transparency which it derives from the French spirit, universal and rational. The Englishman feels the same of his own tongue, except that he is inclined to pride himself upon its non-rationality, and to insist that no language can take root without its meed of idiomatic queerness. As against these positive languages, whose words and phrases have a history and bear the scars of conflict, attraction and erosion, the artificial languages make no headway.

On the other hand, no people can elect its own tongue to be the world-speech and impose it on the world. It is just the deliberate identification of one's own with the absolute that leads to rebellion and to war. (And all wars are in this sense wars of religion.) But there are slow approaches through an indirect route—the spontaneous choices of various peoples of a second language, and the drift toward agreement in these second choices. It is at least conceivable that in this way a particular language might become by silent election a world speech, but without displacing any other speech which, for its own colour, desired to maintain itself.

Through these analogies, the suspicion arises that the particular and local element in religion may be no mere historical accident, but essential to religion itself. To determine this question, we must turn from these analogies to examine the nature of religion.

2

THE NATURE OF RELIGION

WHAT is the nature of this entity, religion, which shows itself in these many particular versions?

Wherever it is found, religion lies close to the roots of human nature; it belongs to the realm of our most elemental will. If, to agree on a name, we were to characterise the deepest impulse in us as a "will to live," religion also could be called a will to live, but with an accent of solicitude—an ambition to do one's living *well*! Or, more adequately, *religion is a passion for righteousness, and for the spread of righteousness, conceived as a cosmic demand.*

Religion is a neighbour of morality, but it is not the same thing. The difference lies first in that factor of "cosmic demand." And then in the depth of feeling: when this cosmic concern fuses with one's own there arises that peculiar ardour for right living which dutifulness alone knows nothing about. For if right living, whatever it is, lies in the nature of things, not simply in my free choice, then whether I go right or not is *not solely my own concern*: the total world, there, expects something of me, and my effort becomes a response; the moral scene acquires, as in binocular vision, a third dimension, a qualitatively new importance.

Religion in this sense is clearly a step out of privacy, a rejection of the illusion of privacy. In a sense, each self is alone with its experience: it issues its acts from a position of complete inner security; it enjoys "subjectivity." And subjectivity is opportunity. All the primitive iniquities—greed, lust, sloth, callousness— are the exploiting of the subjective opportunity in the interest of my private gratification. Religion is the rejection of this exploit from the root, because of an elemental inkling that the privacy is conferred and therefore not absolute: religion is the redemption of solitude.* To interpret life as the great chance to do as I please violates a subtle element of command, the mystical element in primitive experience, which always attends the ethical element.

In this description of religion, two terms require comment:

The term "righteousness" is not used in the conventional sense of compliance with a known law. It is a search for a law: there is a right way of living, it must be found. There is a primitive assurance (will the psychologist explain how it arises?) that living is intended to be good; and an equally primitive denial that living as it offers itself *is* good! There hang over this presented "living," with its spot-plaques of pleasantness and its sporadic evasions of misfortune, the curses of accidentality, passingness, fear. Pleasures and pains, what are they? The quintessence of mean-

---

* *The Meaning of God in Human Experience*, p. 404. Cf. these words from al-Shadhili:

> "I was wont to feel desolate when alone
> But now I revel in loneliness.
> Solitude has become a solace to me,
> Loneliness, too, a precious company."

Translation by E. J. Jurji, *Illumination in Islamic Mysticism*, p. 60.

ing? Conferring meaning on all around? On the contrary, they are riddles: the last thing to be described as "given" is the worth of a spot of pleasure or pain. No quality remains two instants the same: with every change in our perspective, with every item of new knowledge, its value changes. Its worth is the reflection of many things upon its stuff—of time-passage, after-tastes, a million consequences, acquired understanding, the shadow and lightning from the infinite overhanging cloud of selfhood. Worth comes from the penumbra of the spot more than from the spot itself; there is no mature person who would wish to expunge from his experience certain ones of his treasured pains. Thus from the human side, there is an aboriginal postulate: "There must be a way of life, distinct from this, a right way." This bent toward an unknown rightness is the *dikaiosune*, the love of justice of Plato.

The term "passion" also needs comment. It implies here not a disturbed state of emotion but the inescapable urgency or "seriousness" which belongs to the central stake of human existence—whether one lives or misses living. We know we are ignorant; but we know further that we are subject to illusion. There is the illusion of those appealing spot-values we have spoken of; but there is also the illusion of the mystic, who may be caught in some subjective simplification of the whole issue, such as saying with the Stoic that "the conditions of happiness are *within*"—surely a half truth and no more! Between these alternative illusions one may lose—or as the phrase is, be "lost," they are the same. Hence human living proceeds under a tension of concern, anxiety, such as no animal can feel; for it is only the human type of consciousness which knows that living, in its chief dimension, may be a failure. This anxious self-consciousness is the capacity for religion; and the depth of concern is the measure of the man.

Because passion in this radical sense is the medium of religion, all of what comes forward as "truth" in religion is emotionally important. This does not make feeling or emotion the source of religious truth—as if religious truth were a projected wish-fulfilment—which would be another way of defeating all wishes by requiring them to fulfil themselves. But it does imply that no theoretical proposition is true in religion, apart from feeling: the God who is found as a mere fact in the world, or as a cosmological function, is not the God whom religion seeks. Creeds are never mere items of assent; they are by definition the truths of most vital importance, most deeply cared about. No article which is mere doctrine should have any place in a religious creed.

Passion is so far the medium of religion that whatever is of passion tends to be religious. Any enthusiasm relieves man of his paltrier self-concern. Social and humane enthusiams redeem and ennoble their subjects. Hence there is a certain justice in the prevalent judgment that national and social movements are contemporary modes of religion. But they fall short of religion just in so far as they fall short of perceiving the "cosmic demand." They have less right to the name than the passion for truth in science, or the passion for beauty in art—a passion whose power to absorb and transform a personality is too little considered. And beyond these striking "religions" of the social agenda, there is still the more persistent passion for humanity, genuine and concrete, though devoid of the character of a "movement," often appearing as an independent impulse, reaching beyond the religions of party action, and groping outward for a cosmic basis. All of these are inductive movements toward religion, destined to be fragments of religion, incorporated, with their passions, in religion, when religion itself is attained.

Finally, it is not implied in the definition that this passion for righteousness is an unsatisfied hunger. It is an ongoing process sustained by partial success. There is in religion an inalienable kernel of certainty, a sense of rightness of direction which guides the search for more explicit certainty. Religion could properly be defined as man's hold on the absolute and eternal, his rescue from the flux of disorder and futility. But this emphasis on attainment must not conceal the complementary truth that stability must forever recover itself. "What you have inherited, that labour to possess" is the form of religious living. If man had not the eternal he would not be man; nor would he be man if he had the eternal in complete clarity. Eros, as Diotima said, is the child of poverty and plenty: and love, at this point, is the aura of religion.

3

THE TWO POSTULATES

(1) RELIGION MUST BE UNIVERSAL

FROM our conception of religion it follows at once
that religion must be universal. It arises in a universal
human craving directed to an equally universal object.

The passion for righteousness is not a capacity of
special men or races. It belongs to the psychology of
man; that is, it is the response of human nature everywhere as it faces its finite situation in the great world.
This passion is certainly not equally distributed: in
some persons it rises to the point of genius; many
appear dull, and many more acquire dullness to the
total situation, on the plausible plea that we can
neither know nor do anything about it. But there are
no natively unreligious peoples or individuals. The
generic human craving to live as a man is always
there; also the generic ignorance, and with that a
generic anxiety which will not be put down; also a
generic self-respect, with an aboriginal confidence that
the right way of taking the world will not remain
forever hidden from the seeker.

This is a strange trouble and a strange confidence.
The animal neither suffers nor enjoys them. The
animal is factual and positivist; he has no worry about
what he does not know nor understand. The human
being is nowhere merely factual nor positivist except

by a late and artificial simplification of outlook. To the natural man everywhere, the world is fact but also mystery; and to the same natural man this mystery is no final blankness but an invitation.

There is a purely biological confidence which goes with every instinctive desire. The desire for food carries with it the working assumption that food exists in the environment; the infant animal takes for granted what the biologist in due time confirms—that no vital desire could stand for a general physical futility. But the peculiar equipment of desires which marks the human species carries with it no such biological warrant; the desire to know the nature of things, to gain a just sense of their qualities, and the like, need not be satisfied in order that the human species may survive. Yet man carries over into this realm also his biological confidence; religion is a hopeful passion, and even where fear and awe predominate, this hope (tinged with a sense of right) is also universal.

Further, the object which will satisfy this universal craving, the right way, is taken by men everywhere to be a universal object; an absolute, in the sense that it holds good for all men in all places at all times. This statement requires some confirming; since the very fact of mystery and difficulty lends to the search the character of individual adventure and individual finding, such finding as might conceivably be a private triumph and a happy secret.* But while the effort and

---

* To say that there is an "art of life" or a "way of life" and that religion is the will to find and to live according to this art, is true. But the phrases are images of external arts, and when taken literally, trivialise the truth they express.

For to say there is an "art" or a "way" sets one searching for a technique,

the attainment must be individual, what one attains has the quality of "truth," valid for all men.

It is for this reason that religion, in its normal effect, unites men rather than divides them. To be actively concerned for an absolute end is the indirect road to human unity, more certain than the direct road—at bottom the only road to unity.

Human beings can only approach each other by way of *third* objects. We do not see each other; we see only the outer shell—the body, and the objects which we have in common—things and events in space. We are like persons on opposite sides of a mountain, invisible to one another; they cannot meet by direct approach, they have nothing to aim at, but each can see along his own path the point of junction, the rendezvous; by way of this third object they meet. Likewise with all mental approach. There is no direct

a psychological recipe, a prescription, a professional secret, a sacred Yoga, a mystery, a solemnly private initiation, a cavern of magic. In this vein, the quest for elixirs of life or for philosophers' stones or for Holy Grails or for medicines of immortality sent many early-eager minds on long voyages or deep into the detective business of nature's infinite subtleties. Religion learns slowly that it cannot be contained in any artfulness nor happy discovery nor wilfully privileged whisper of Deity, nor surprised sacred secret.

All the emotional interests of the figures are valid: there is mystery, discovery, adventurous Pilgrim's Progress, a treasure hid in a field to be jealously and shrewdly pre-empted. All this, as a figure; but the figure signifies a natural obstacle and effort: living well is not a given fact but only a possibility; and the guide to this possibility is a faint native sense of direction, whose reading requires the most faithful and sensitive attention, and a stern moral cost. The elements of secret and of adventure are but metaphors for the growing difficulty of reading aright this subtle direction-ality, the increasing demand for moral rectitude as a condition of knowledge, and so, the ever closer dependence of men upon those who have been able to accept the severe conditions of another step forward. There is no intrinsic hiddenness, no possible proprietary nostrum, no key-possessing sinecure.

way of comparing ideas and sentiments; agreement means a common attitude to a common object; ultimate agreement means caring for and serving the same causes—worshipping the same gods. All human approach of minds and wills is thus indirect.

And the only men fit to lead others are those who have their own hold on this third entity, the god, or the real. They are the only ones who can lead others, who reach their judgments with no eye on the spectator, but only on the object. In their unsocial drive to the independent verity, such men are more social than those who trim their thoughts to suit their neighbours. Augustine in his *Soliloquies*, or Descartes in his *Meditations*, become in their solitude the companions of the centuries because their thoughts converse with a being, real for all men.

Religion thus contains in itself the ultimate truth of human psychology (not, as a rule, discovered by the psychologists),* that the mental life of man is

* The temptation of psychology is to set up a subjective equivalent for religion, in which the objects are indifferent. Thus, the cure of souls proceeds on findings of psychiatry or psycho-analysis, in lofty disregard of the supernaturalism of traditional religion: psychology will thus put religion on a "scientific" basis. The proffered help of the Buddha or of the Christ may be graciously declined, for "salvation" now means "integration" or "release" or "sublimation" . . . and the Confessional is simplified (?) into a procedure of technical self-disgorgery. This was an experiment worth trying; and its discovery is that the omission of the religious object does not do. Modern man as Jung has discerned, must resume connection with his "soul," and what, pray, is that? It is simply the self, concerned with its realities, its objects of widest scope, its absolutes. The self cannot be cut off from its object, as a "state of mind," and remain anything at all.

The psychology of religion is a discipline well calculated to see the identity between diverse symbols, on the principle that whatever symbolisms establish the same mental states are the same in meaning, or have elements of sameness. This use requires not a psychology without objects, but one in which the mental state is a clue to its object.

conversation with an absolute object, apart from which the whole sail-expanse of his several desires flaps loosely and variously in divergent winds. And since this is everywhere the case, religion contains the release from all localism, and from all historical accidents. It crosses every boundary between man and man, and between the earliest man and the latest in time. It is the farthest reach of universality of which the race is capable.

4

THE TWO POSTULATES

(2) RELIGION MUST BE PARTICULAR

THE result we have reached seems to carry with it the cancellation of the particular and separative aspects of religion. On the contrary, it requires them.

For the fact that any religious finding is universal carries with it an impulse to communicate it. And communication is never to human beings in general: it is to specific human beings, having specific difficulties in seeing what is meant, having specific languages and histories with whatever resources of legend and reflection are there to be drawn upon for explanation, also with specific ethical and social questions to meet. If it were only as a pedagogical necessity, it must assume the peculiar mental and moral burdens of that time and place, and so become coloured by their idiosyncrasies.

Because religion is universal, it must become particular.

This general truth, since its understanding will affect our whole attitude toward the relations of the specific religions, must be dwelt upon in some detail.

That religion tends to communicate itself will be asserted by any observer of religious psychology. In so far as the passion for righteousness reaches satisfaction, it becomes a passion for the spread of righteousness. And this activity of spreading, as well as the search for and the practice of the right way, is conceived as a cosmic demand.

This impulse lies at the root of much unique religious behaviour whose meaning tends to escape the polite academic mind, for example, the strange activity of preaching, which naturally expands into the founding of a religious community with its special organisation, and into the mission.

Why, we must ask, should religion, the most inward, secret, inaccessible of all concerns—"the flight of the alone to the Alone"—try to make itself public? Publicity is an offence to religion; to be observed is hateful to the true worshipper and to every group of true worshippers, who are precisely *not* observers of one another.

Hegel has a simple answer, worth noting for a certain characteristic high-handed finality. "The Spirit," he says, "must give itself existence!" To this dogmatic mystery we may attempt to lend some light. Perhaps this: everything in the realm of "spirit"—thought, fancy, feeling—tries to take on bodily form: we can hardly think at all unless our ideas wrap themselves in floating imagery, then attach themselves to words, then work themselves into action. A "mere idea" is next to nothing, an aching emptiness; it is like an invisible wind which aspires to be a whirlwind, taking up enough grit and stubble to career as a thing among things! An "idea" is just a piece of the ultimate reality which is "spirit"; and the tug of the idea to take visible shape, its nisus to substantialise itself, is our most intimate evidence of the nature of all such reality—to become "concrete." If we may translate Hegel in this way, his dictum is valid, and goes deep. Religion, let us say, is nothing but the reality in man behaving according to its most natural law. And whatever seems strange about religion seems so only because it is strange to us to be radically natural. Hegel is right; but he speaks with the vague gesture of a poet who lacks the concreteness he points to. We want a more explicit and contemporary psychology: why must "Spirit give itself existence" in just this manner?

Some light we find in the fact that religion belongs to the realm of passion; and that passion lives like fire by giving itself away. Further, it is a passion which shapes conduct; and since conduct is visible to others, and is always read as a sign of its motive, there will be no concealment of any distinctive intent in the behaviour of the religious man. The words of Gregory Thaumaturgos about Origen are an eloquent tribute to this kind of involuntary communication:

> His words were so kind and affectionate that love sprang up in my soul as if kindled by a spark; love not only for him, but for all that is good, and for the divine Logos of whom he is the friend and advocate. He incited us to virtue much more by what he did than by what he said. The sum of all his teaching and example was this: Be pure in mind, and so become like God that you may draw near Him and abide in Him.*

* Version of Rev. A. E. Teale.

But religion commonly calls for a more deliberate kind of self-expression. An example outside our own tradition:

> Korozumi Muneteda (1780–1850) as a young man heard lectures on the Shinto texts; like some other theological students he found them wooden. As he put it, "Nothing was said in them of the wonderful power of divinity, of the response between man and deity, of the profound principles of the soul." He aspired to be a *kami*—literally, a "spirit," but as applied to men, a "renewer of faith." To this end he undertook "three great worships." In one of these, while engaged in devotion to Amaterasu Omikami, the sun goddess, he suddenly felt (so his account runs) "his spirit expand with unwonted exhilaration . . . and he had communion with the life-principle of Nature . . . and laid hold on Living Being, Iki Mono." Along with this he felt he had received a divine commission to share with others the happiness that had come to him.*

Enlightenment which has come after a long struggle can hardly fail to have this impulsive quality. There is an element of duty in the situation which coincides with the natural impulse of joy to overflow. This duty is pointed and personal: it is the attainer who must speak. These motives have their most marked classical expression in the experience of the Buddha; after he had won through his Enlightenment the right to enter into peace, he was tempted by the Devil to do so, as by the pure logic of his system he should have done: but (recognising pure logic in this case as the Devil in disguise?), he chose, out of compassion for men, to remain among them as a preacher of his Gospel.

There is another motive in this situation. Unless

* D. C. Holtom and Honaga, *Some Modern Sects of Shinto.*

the discoverer speaks, he is separated from his fellows by his insight, rather than united to them., His enlightenment is socially dangerous. Its difficulty tends to set him off as follower of an esoteric insight; he is the mystic, a man not wholly articulate. If he claims to be the bearer of a divine revelation, he is not on this account either loved or trusted. The man with a private god has always been feared: his deepest emotions diverge from those of his fellows. His truth is potentially the deepest bond of himself with his fellows; but *unless they see that truth*, it alienates him from them. It is not a bond unless it is *made a bond*: he must become a teacher, or else a hermit or an outcast.

As a matter of biography, the great mystics have inclined to alternate in the roles of teacher and hermit.

Religion establishes the self-sufficiency of the individual soul in its relation to God: in theory, the mystic needs no human associate; hermitude is the experimental demonstration of his inner achievement. Yet even in Hinduism, the most individualist of all religions, the hermit customarily leaves a path to his door!

> This path is the confession of his incompleteness as a religious individual. I remember my surprise in seeking out, in India, the retreat of a pundit who had been a student of Yoga, and who had taken the vows of the sannyasi. He was to be sought in the region near Lakhsmansjula, beyond Rishikesh, where the Ganges emerges cold and swift from the Himalayas. I passed over the swinging bridge across the Ganges gorge, the bridge which gives Lakhsmansjula its name, and then turning downstream followed a path above the river for a few miles until it

led into an open shelf deeply recessed into the mountains. Here on this table of fertile earth, well treed and gardened, I found my sannyasi. But he was in the midst of a *colony of sannyasis!* There was a temple for common prayer and instruction. There were establishments for the issuance of food, prepared according to the scriptural recipes. And here was my friend, acting as medical adviser to ailing sannyasis. A colony of hermits! Some of them indeed vowed to silence. All of them spending many hours in seclusion; each having his own cabin, from which the world could be locked out. But each within reach of the other, each one a member of the simple social organisation thrown over the whole group, and all accessible to such of mankind as would take the trouble to seek them out. And though the hermit who burns his bridges, and follows the sacred precept to move steadfastly through the sacred mountains and their snows in a north-easterly direction until he parts company with this sphere of illusion, may exist, he must at least be known to have disappeared; and my judgment is that there are very few such. The instinct of religious solitude is to hold its fruits as gifts for a future human society.

And there are not wanting signs that the higher religious sense rejects even a moral self-sufficiency. There are signs that the mystic feels at times that salvation cannot be complete in solitude—as if the sin and lostness of other men penetrated one's own security. Such signs are surprising in religions which profess a doctrine of Karma, which asserts the perfect independence of the moral destiny of each individual thread of life. Yet they are there.

We recall the story of thirteenth-century Nichiren, Japanese prophet of a type of Buddhism based on the Lotus Sutra. Nichiren held the strong conviction that national

calamities are consequences of general sinfulness; and that
the mission of the religious prophet is thus, in part, national
—he has to ward off public perils by correcting the errors
of religious conception prevalent in his time. His own task
was to displace the spurious types of Buddhism (Jodo,
Shingon, Amita), and to set in their place the one pure
type, the "Adoration of the Lotus of Perfect Truth." This
strong sense of mission he expressed in the famous three-
fold vow contained in the essay Kaimoku-shō (Opening
of the Eyes): "I will be the Pillar of Japan; I will be the
Eyes of Japan; I will be the Great Ship of Japan." But he
was already an exile when he wrote these words (1272);
his preaching had been rejected; the advance of Kublai
Khan had begun to threaten the peace of the Islands;
tribute had been demanded. The public sufferings and his
own confirmed his belief: the people had sinned, and he
also was responsible, for he *had not convinced* them! His
exile was a part of his expiation. If the nation was indifferent to his preaching, he had failed in his personal duty.

In more recent times, we recall the logic by which
Gandhi has been accustomed to impose fasts upon
himself as expiation of the sins of his followers: if
he has not convinced them, there has been something
inadequate, he argues, in his own witness to the truth.

In the West we find less frequently the striking and
separate assertion that "the sins of these others are my
sins," because our sense of life is more frittered and sub-
divided. Yet here, too, the logic makes itself felt. John
Jay Chapman, man of letters, native of New York,
made a few years ago a strange journey to the village of
Coatesville, Pennsylvania. This village in the previous
year had been the scene of the lynching of a negro, a
crime which the northern states of our country have
commonly held as a reproach against our southern states.
Chapman felt the disgrace of this northern lynching as

attaching to the entire region in which his life had been placed, and to him personally. On the anniversary of the event, he announced a penitential service in Coatesville, inviting the members of that unrepentant community to attend. He carried through the service with one other person present.

Unquestionably the religious impulse in its more powerful representatives lifts personality into a region where the walls of moral isolation between man and man wear thin. And where such a sense of community in sinfulness exists, it must lend a deeper gravity to the disposition to spread righteousness. And in so far as one's moral destiny becomes thus identified with the moral destiny of the group within which one acts, the religion of the preacher will be immersed in regional character and regional history: it will be religion in particular.

But we have still to realise the full force of the need which the active religious spirit has for its community. It is as though the mystic (for so we may name for brevity the man who is touched by religion), emerging from the community and freeing himself from its localisms through grasp of the absolute, then found himself somehow in need of that very community with all its particular marks in order to complete his religious selfhood.

5

THE MYSTIC NEEDS THE COMMUNITY

THE inner light brings its own certitude and self-sufficiency. One of the functions of God in society is to make a man capable of being alone, independent of other men. Yet this independent individual, the mystic, shows a disposition not alone to preach to others, but to gather around himself disciples and to make them a stable, growing group, building a community within the community on his own principle of living.

Why does he do this? We understand that an idea does not belong to the man who "has" it; its destiny is to be mounted in the lives of all those who can use it. Its life is outside his head, not alone within it, and he, the owner, becomes its servant. But why does he try to build a group?

Does he need any external corroboration? In his desire to give is there a subconscious need to assure himself that his ideas are givable, ergo valid? Did Buddha have an unconfessed need of his hearers, and of just those hearers who had earlier forsaken him? Did Socrates need his young friends and auditors? Did Jesus need his disciples? Have we here an instance of that paradoxical and yet not uncommon neediness of the self-sufficient, as when a character proud and complete finds itself lonely, and therefore in some sense futile.

I think there is a bit of truth in this suggestion,

rather perversely put. It is not that the mystic confirms in his disciples what he is already sure of; it is rather the negative side of this—if he had no capacity to persuade, he would have to suspect himself. Ideas and feelings which have no power over other minds are either subjective or falsely defined: the presence of his group is the continued experimental corroboration (and development) both of his truth and of his way of putting it to work.

But this is an incidental and partial answer.

Beyond this there is another need, due to the fact that the search for righteousness is *continuous*. The mystic comes out of a community which was before him and will be after him. His own search for righteousness is a continuation of the life of that community. He returns to this life with his new truth: he has a need to see it incorporated in that particular ongoing historical process.

For truth is never truth in general; it is answer to question. Now questioning is historical; or to put it conversely, the history of any group is a corporate questioning process. Each community has its own frontier of perception, its own region of groping. It has what we may call its world-line of religious searching.

The line of religious and moral effort is drawn for each group in a different place. Thus Islam has not tried from the first to root out polygamy, nor fighting and raiding, nor to reach perfection anywhere; nevertheless it has defined its own moral issues, and its achievements in securing regularity and abstemiousness within these lines are astonishing. The good Moslem is a good citizen and a reliable man: English residents of the Malay Peninsula are not as a rule eager to alter the faith of their million and a half Moslems. Hinduism has its own moral frontier, not that of Islam, and not ours. And so for the other religions.

Now the mystic is a bearer in his own person of the questioning out of which he was born. When he joins his community in worship, he joins in its questioning —for worship when it is alive contains a new groping of the soul, not a wearing deeper of old ruts. And if he finds an answer, he must bring it back into the context of the questioning to which the answer applies. He must vest his insight in that particular historical campaign.

But there is a third need, and perhaps the deepest one, the need which belongs to the nature of religion as feeling.

As feeling, religion takes the shape, for the community, of ritual. Of this side of religion we have had little to say. Of the three sides of religion—creed, code, ritual—ritual appears the least significant. As the nesting place for all that is magical, the reflective consciousness is commonly mystified and offended by it. Yet it is just these ritual elements which, as anthropologists know, are the most enduring elements of a religion.* Ceremonial implements and habits are the

---

* Observance is the lasting element of the concrete religions. This is not due to the fact that ritual objects are hard and do not decay. This is indeed a fortunate item for the anthropologist, and an incidental testimony to the

sole relics of many a forgotten faith; the sign of the Cross persists where creed and code are out of mind, and the manner of making it marks, to many a Roman Catholic or Orthodox believer, the chief criterion of his Church.

When Dr. Hendrik Kraemer, after much effort, gained permission from the Dutch Government to open a Christian mission in Bali, he went with the wish and intent to preserve as much as possible of the charm of the native ways. He thought that most of what was characteristic could remain, as consonant with Christianity: the Balinese thought otherwise. Many of them were open to persuasion; but to them a religion was less something to believe than something to do. It was a special way of dealing with birth, marriage, death. Hence to change religion meant—not to change creeds and keep customs, but to change customs and let creeds take the consequences. Observance was close to the essence of religion.

And indeed, is it not in observance that we find the most conspicuous insignia of the particular religions—including in this term with the modes of public worship and ceremony, the sacraments, the music, the modes of architecture and vestment, the orders of the religious life? Men are divided everywhere far less by creeds than by ritual. Why has it this peculiar importance?

aboriginal nature of religious ideas. But ritual objects are hard, and are chosen as such, because they are employed in the function of conserving, of recurrent use, or of serving the dead through a lasting future. The offering is consumed, but the altar and its vessels remain. Gold and jade come into religious employment long before they attain value in commerce.

It is, I suggest, because feeling is important, and because ritual is the vessel of communal feeling. If we say that feeling is our cognizance of value, or that feeling is the report of consciousness that value is present, it becomes a truism that without feeling life is valueless. But feeling, the most important element of experience, is also the most intangible. It cannot be conveyed from mind to mind in its own character: its expression is necessarily in another medium, in space, form, sound, grimace, gesture. All of these expressions are "irrational" in the sense that they could not be deduced from the feeling itself; and in the further sense that they cannot be rationally read —if they are "understood" it must be by a sympathy which is carried along in a specific biological and social current. There are indeed some elements in religious expression which approach universality: attitudes of reverence and supplication are much the same everywhere, but these are invariably enswathed in a mass of usages purely local and unintelligible to the alien eye.

Further, feeling is *evanescent*. It is quicksilver; the worth of life runs down; it cannot be held by force, nor recovered by the will to recall. This is the despair of all self-conscious living—the decline of the emotional energy which sustains the will: be it love of friend, hatred of enemy, ambition, moral resolve, the spell of beauty, the gusto of the epicure, the joy of sport, the morale of an arduous campaign, the zest of life itself—how shall these priceless essences be preserved? Religious feeling, underlying all others, is in the same case; it, too, runs down; savedness does not last; the passion for righteousness requires to be renewed.

Now all efforts to seize on feeling as if it were a substance, and to hold on to it, are futile. The lover may be horrified to note his love ebbing; but when the will to love becomes a loyal substitute for love itself, feeling is gone. But neither love nor any other feeling was originally gained by being directly aimed at, nor ever in its flood taken as a separate entity: feeling is a natural response to the meaning found in an actual situation. And all sound feeling sets up its own plan of renewal by reminder of the original situation, or by reinstating the ideas or thoughts which originally aroused it. How often does life establish its own private and pathetic rituals; one thinks to recover an old rapture by revisiting the scene of its origin! This is the sense of pilgrimage, the visit to the "Holy Land."

And this is the essential nature of all observance— *the cumulative conservation of feeling*, through the establishment of adequate expressive signs, steeped in the accidents of the history of that feeling. Through the rituals, the pertinent feelings of the race are conserved at their height, and are placed at the disposal of individuals in those crises of experience in which solitary emotion falters.

Individual feeling indeed seldom reaches its normal level in solitude; the group lends it dimension, stability, sanction, standard, conceptual structure, imaginative scope. Still less is it able to retain such a level. And here we see again that the mystic needs the community. He can only conserve his own emotion by vesting it in community observance, where it can reflect to him, through local symbols, the adequate response of mankind to the inner glory of the world.

He needs the community, we have said, for the placing of his thought in the world-line of questioning, and for the preservation of his feeling. He needs it also for the *prolongation of his deed*. The spread of righteousness is a task which cannot be limited by the reach of an individual either in space or in time. So far as his "work" deserves to continue, it can continue beyond his personal scope only if there is a community to continue it. It may conceivably extend his sway over the minds and feelings of men to a possible eternity, and thus provide him an immortality of deed on earth.

It is not that the mystic foresees and intends these various supplementations of his finite selfhood as he conveys his idea; it is we who, tracing effects and causes, see by what inevitable instinct his universal thought and passion enter the local texture of a present community process.

6

THE COMMUNITY NEEDS THE MYSTIC

W HILE the mystic is building up his own inner group, as a sort of leaven within the wider secular community, this wider community relies on such work as his for certain qualities which it cannot produce for itself. The two reciprocal needs which thus meet tie the religious product closer to the historical group with all its local peculiarities.

The secular community cannot live without "morale" on the part of its citizens; that is, they must be *disposed* to accept the purposes and principles of state action. No state can constrain all its citizens all the time, nor even any large fraction of them a large part of the time. It depends not alone on prevalent acceptance of its will, but on a certain positive fund of faith in its total character. Now this spontaneous consent of the citizen within his citizenship the state can signalise and sustain by its own ceremonial observances, but not create.

Consider, for example, the feelings implied in the punishment of crime. It is assumed in the sentimental conventions of the courts that these feelings are always available. They are not. Any state can announce punishments, but punishments do not punish unless they are at the same time condemnations. And they are not condemnations unless the emotional severity of the community is with them. When the culprit is half-blamed and half-admired, at once reprobate and hero, target of gaze for a morally obtuse public, patrons of an obtuser press, the meaning has leaked out of punishment. And the point is, *the community cannot restore it.* Somewhere, the edifice of emotions must rest on a foundation of unconstrained seriousness. Religion is the name of this foundation. Without religion, or the emotional traces of past religion, the state is powerless to punish crime. The community depends for its indispensable morale upon the mystic and his findings.

It depends upon the same source for those special servants whose devotion to its interest exceeds what any laws could require. No state can survive unless there is a group of able men ready to spend themselves in its behalf far beyond any definable duty; and the measure of its greatness is in the stature of such men. Their will to public service must come from the resources of their own loneliness; religion is the name for these resources.

Hence, for the sake of its own daily necessities, the community is bound to abet the honest life of its independent religious groups. And for the severer crises of its experience no state has anything better to do than to secure those positive feelings which are able to support such strains—its patriotisms, its love of justice, its righteous angers. All of these feelings are natural and spontaneous; and all of them are fickle with the fickleness of natural passion. If they are to be relied on, they must have beneath them the constant warrant of validity—they must be derived

from the primary passion for righteousness. The community must cultivate its mystics.

The community, when it has a choice, cannot avoid
exercising a selective influence on its religion: it
cannot dictate how men shall worship God (though
it has attempted it), but having a choice among
mystics and their followers, it cannot but weight its
favour toward that mode of religion which is most
nearly in harmony with its own moral direction. Thus
China, having Confucius, Lao Tze, Moh Ti, chooses
Confucius; India having Buddha and the Puranas
chooses the Puranas, while Buddhism is exported to
East and North; Palestine of the first century, having
orthodox Judaism and the cult of Jesus, chooses
Judaism, while Christianity moves North and West.
By virtue of this undemonstrative selective action the
dominance of any religion in any place means a degree
of incorporation with the local culture: the adoption
is mutual.

Religion has always recognised the moral peril of
this situation; to say that it has always escaped political dictation or more subtle political bribery would
be preposterous; what we can say is that it has always
striven to maintain its own autonomy and primacy.
But at the very least, it assumes some responsibility
for saving the secular community, and not individuals
alone. And in so doing, its observances take on the
colours of the historical situation, its habits and emotional idiosyncrasy. Religion, by its social involvement,
becomes particularised.

7

THE DILEMMA OF RELIGION

Religion must be universal; religion must be particular. If our reflections have been just, religion cannot become the ideal of the philosophers and saints, a pure communion of the individual soul with the absolute and true, a spirit devoid of body, universal by its very conception. It must live as a fact in the world by dint of its own nature. And the dilemma that results is in part the inherent conflict between the freedom of universality, and the limitation of the particular. In part, it is a conflict between the sober rationality of the universal and the element of the irrational which enters with the particular. We speak first of this aspect of irrationality.

Those who think about religion are apt to underrate the importance of feeling, and its expression; because of this, I shall dwell on it. It is hard to realise the momentum of a deep emotional current, and its boundary-making force. But the inherent queerness of emotional expression we can at least call to mind.

Picture a night of full moon in Bombay, the great disc directly overhead; worshippers assembled in the courtyard of a temple, chanting together a song of Rama, under the leadership of a priest. In another court, women seated in a circle under an arched roof; a number of them rise to take part in a sacred dance to the music of flute and drum; the dancers move in

a circle with rhythmic stamping; the many bodies
become part of a single moving pattern, and the many
minds flow into a unity of feeling palpably real: there
is a gradual increase of speed; the name "Rama" is
sounded at regular intervals of the rhythm; drum and
cry increase in volume with the increase of speed;
finally the leader of the dance begins to swing the
great kalaldrom, and the dance ends in a violent crash
of sound.

Picture a night in Cairo, during the fast-month of
Ramadan. A slow irregular procession forms in a
side street; its members are undistinguished people,
workmen, shopkeepers, sweepers, young and old; it
moves toward a square facing an old palace, now
headquarters of certain dervish orders. As it reaches
this spot, toward midnight, it assumes a degree of
formality and draws itself up before the palace steps;
it is met here by the chief men of the order. There is
a responsive chant of stanzas from the Koran. Coffee
is served; and shortly the members range themselves
in two rows facing one another, musicians at one end
of the double line; a low chant begins—again of lines
from the Koran. The lines are repeated several times,
and then changed; with the chanting a swaying of the
body backward and forward, increasing slightly in
tempo and in vigour. Some of the older singers with-
draw. With the remaining members the music of the
Zikr goes on to a climax of fervour; after the summit
a sudden moment of silence and, as it seems, of joyful,
perhaps ecstatic, peace. Then the group quietly dis-
perses.

Picture the ceremonies of attending and dressing

the god in an Indian temple; or the running song, lament, and imprecatory prayers of Jewish rabbis in Galicia; or the solemn procession in an Orthodox basilica; or the bleak "Communion" in a Primitive Methodist chapel; or the "heuil" of the Gaelic preacher; or the emotional shouts of victory in a negro service of penitence and redemption.

This queerness of emotional expression is not different in principle from the queerness of the animal body itself. No body feels queer to its owner, until it becomes the object of an external and unsympathetic gaze. But there is a sort of instinctive anticipation of this critical judgment in the shyness with which each religious type protects from just this alien inspection its ceremonial. There is a pseudo-shame which avoids or angrily expels the intruder. A Winnebago Indian, educated at Yale, where he was accustomed to rehearse the folk-stories of his people, returned to his tribe, and was dismayed to find that its ritual gatherings were closed to him, not through hostility, but through a shrinking from a gaze which had become the gaze of an altered personality.

The practical outflow of this feeling about feeling is to insulate the divergent types of emotional expression from one another, and so to confirm the localisms which, on its rational side, religion tends to overcome.

The religion of the American negroes is nominally the religion of the whites. In many ways the treatment of the negro Christians of parts of America has resembled the treatment of the Untouchables in India in the point of their lack of welcome in the temples of the ruling caste. But meantime, they have built their own; and there have cultivated their own expression of the common faith. What I now see in the negro churches of the South is the growth of a distinctive type of emotional expression, far richer and freer than that which obtains in our decorous and intellectualised ritual. They will preserve for Christianity some of the emotional gamut which Protestantism elsewhere loses by its bleaching and dry decay. And as this becomes obvious to themselves, they will insist on maintaining the emotional freedom which is theirs solely by the fact of separation.

Whatever is actual is contaminated by its actuality. For the universal can never lend its full sanction to any particular; the actual shape runs over and beyond its meaning, introducing the arbitrary, the weird and wayward forms, the material slag, the irrelevant claims and motives of the context, the defects of history. The price of existence must be paid; and this price is, to be forever beyond the reach of rational deducibility. To *lack* existence is a fatal defect, never compensated by the inherent beauty of the pure ideal; to *have* existence is to assume the burden of an infinitely extraneous specification.

The price of existence must be paid. We shall not arrive at the world faith by omitting the particulars. The desire of the philosopher to be quit of them, to expunge the apparatus and the circumstance, the pageantry, the reminiscences of savagery, the relics of primitive rifery which cling to almost every higher cult, the phallicisms, the circumcisions, the orgies and intoxications—this desire can be granted in degree—for frenzy will always platonise and mitigate itself toward the contemporary sense of decorum—but not in principle.

Nor can the philosopher be better served when he demands the excision of the human organisation with its personnel, its comfortable livings, its pious frauds, its human fallibilities masquerading as divine decrees, its pretences to possess supernatural secrets and royal roads to privilege in the dark world beyond. The organisation is always the breeding nest of those corruptions which most beget repulsion in the flavour of the word "religion." It makes a pernicious partnership with all that can feed human fear and credulity; it establishes a vicious circle with superstition. A supernatural specific provides the organisation with its most palpable *raison d'être*; the organisation, in turn, protects the supernatural specific from the tests of experience and reason. Thus the most earthly aspect of the religion constitutes itself the authoritative interpreter of its most spiritual part. But the certain cure for all this is simply "enlightenment"—scientific, of course, but also and chiefly the slowly increasing sureness of a sounder religious sense.* It is not to elimin-

* In my own judgment, there is usually more to be lost than gained by the third method of cure—the specific attack upon persons and hierarchies which fall into particular venalities, demagogueries, power-policies, diplomatic knaveries. There are few institutions in the world to-day, since reformations and revolutions have done their surgery, so corrupt that they cannot be cured from within by their own healthful elements better than by piecemeal and partisan hostilities from outside, with their painful aroma of self-righteousness, and their progeny of recrimination, malice, and open sores.

ate organisation, and thus to reduce religion to the scattered embodiment it can find in individual careers.

If, then, religion must be particular and also universal, we appear to have an unresolvable conflict on our hands.

If the worshipper must always join his community and his race in worship, the Hindu is justified in adhering to his Hinduism, as Gandhi insists on doing. The Chinese ought not to dissociate himself from Confucianism, nor the Arab from Islam. Nor ought any of these particular and historic religions—so the argument seems to require—seek to impose itself on any other: it cannot be the historic and local religion for any other group. The same reasons that lead it to insist on its own historic character must lead it to desist from the aim to become "the" world faith. If we cannot understand a civilisation without its religion, how can we understand a religion without the civilisation it has formed? And since civilisations cannot simply substitute themselves one for another, the concept of a concrete world-faith seems to be excluded by our results.

At the same time, no religion alive to its own meaning can surrender the assumption of its destiny to remain concrete and to be universal.

In presence of this unresolved dilemma, the living religions fall into two groups, those which put foremost the functions of religion as particular, and those which put foremost its functions as universal—those which accept localism as their meaning and destiny, and those which adhere to the postulate that religion must be universal, and that they are that religion.

Hinduism, Confucianism, Shinto, Judaism (with some caveat), have accepted the local limitation which their names indicate. Each one of them is wrapped up with the mores of its own community. Hinduism is identified with the social system of India; Judaism with the laws and customs of the Jewish people. All such systems undergo processes of change; the religion is in part the ferment inducing such change, and in part accepts change initiating in the social experience of the people. All of them regard doctrine as incidental to behaviour: Judaism, like Hinduism, is strikingly tolerant to varieties of metaphysical speculation. This appears as a mark of laudable hospitality of mind: in reality it is a mark of a different conception of religion —the centre of gravity does not lie in creed but in practice. Gandhi has made us familiar with the defence of regional responsibility in religion; however much he appropriates Christian ideas, he remains immovably Hindu: God, he says, has placed him by birth among the Hindus, and there must be his destiny in this life. For the same reason (with exceptions to be noted) none of these religions is now actively missionary.

On the other hand, three of the great religions, Buddhism, Christianity, and Islam, have arisen as reforms, aimed explicitly at overcoming the localism of just such religions as these—two of them, Buddhism and Christianity obviously, as reforms of just these— the Hinduism and Judaism of their day.

They were all efforts to throw off an incubus, that

of the particularities of religion gone corrupt. Islam faced a far less developed system of thought than did the others. Christianity and Buddhism, may be interpreted as rebellions against "a" religion, in the name of religion in its pure universal essence.

They were revolted precisely by the pretence of authority, whether in Brahmin or Scribe, at the local perquisites and ceremonial meshwork, maintained by priestly sinecure and administrative monopoly of the way to God. They have all made for simplification both of thought and of ritual. Buddhism and Christianity have made for "inwardness" of righteousness, as against any ceremonial observance. All have brought the religious code nearer to the natural ethical conscience, and have curtailed the cumbersome mechanism of public observance. All have declared (more or less clearly) against the barriers of social position, caste, sex, race, nation. All had, and continue to have, a consciousness of world-mission.

But there are three such claimants. And they have one further character in common. Each, beginning with a minimum of the particular and local, has fallen into a new particularity. This has occurred in each case through the reference of the universalised teaching of the founder to him, his person, his words and deeds, his place in time and in history, as a part of the object of the cult. It has occurred also through the elaborations of the original simple code as the new movement found itself in special circumstances; and through assuming the burdens of the local civilisations through which it spread. Each has set up a new absolute authority and canon of scripture, about which has grown an elaborate literature. And each has become encrusted with apparatus more complex than any preceding cult—with the possible exception of Hinduism—had dreamed of.

Is this experience a sign of the failure of the notion of the founders that a pure and unparticular religion was possible? Is it a perversion that must again be overcome in the interest of the world faith they dreamed of? Or is it an evidence that in the nature of the idea of religion, the particular must be kept together with the universal?

Part of the answer certainly is this: that the emancipation of mankind from the particular *is itself a particular event*; and mankind remains bound to the celebration of that deed of liberation. And of this situation it is mere folly to say with Kierkegaard that here "reason commits suicide in passion." On the contrary, it is the fulfilment of both reason and passion that the liberating idea takes upon itself existence, in some here and now; and the event is the occasion for earthly and heavenly joy.

But there are three such religions!

8

THE CLASSIFICATION OF RELIGIONS

THE dilemma of religion has pointed to us a mode of classifying the existing religions which, for our purpose, is fundamental. They have arrayed themselves, with such discomfort as always attends a closeting of living things, in three groups:

(a) The predominantly local or ethnic;

(b) The predominantly universal, arising by an attempt to escape the bonds of the local;

(c) The historical-universal, i.e., the universal newly particularised by reference to their own emancipation from particularity, as historic fact.

At this point, a way out of our difficulty may be indicated by introducing another principle of classification. The religions may be divided into the revealed and the non-revealed. The revealed religions are those of the semitic group, Judaism, Islam, Christianity, the "religions of the Book," in the Moslem phrase. The religions of eastern Asia are, in contrast, religions in which man, by discipline and reflective effort, wins his own enlightenment, and finds salvation thereby. These religions, especially Hinduism and Buddhism, are gigantic monuments of human prowess, moral and philosophical. Even their authoritative scriptures are regarded as the work of great seers, rather than the authentic revealed will of God. When they come into direct comparison with the religions of revelation, they must—the inference is—naturally give way.

And of these religions of revelation, Judaism—so the proposers of this classification usually argue—is superseded by or absorbed into Christianity; whereas Islam—so they continue—is a poorly edited adaptation of the other two to the needs of a desert people, which should probably be regarded as a very impeded revelation, or perhaps (to employ the words of a distinguished German theologian) as "*ueberhaupt keine Offenbarung*"—no revelation at all! This arrangement very neatly leaves Christianity as the one legitimate vessel of the world faith. Perhaps too neatly?

We shall have to deal directly with the concept of revelation. For those who can believe that God has spoken to Moses as he has not spoken to men in other lands who have hungered and thirsted after righteousness, so that the Beatitude of Jesus to the effect that such "shall be filled" was false teaching, this may be the simple and direct solution of all problems. For those who can believe this there is, in fact, no problem about the world faith: the classification as often happens contains the *parti pris* which is the conclusion.

We shall not assume that they are wrong; nor in advance of our own enquiry shall we assume that they are right. In the meantime it would certainly be a matter of shame rather than of congratulation if the only evidence for the finality of our faith were its supernatural origin, and the only evidence for its supernatural origin were our faith.

LECTURE II
SOME CHARACTERISTICS
OF ORIENTAL RELIGIONS

SOME CHARACTERISTICS OF ORIENTAL RELIGIONS

ORDINARILY, our first knowledge of Oriental religions is gained from western expositors. In a hundred and fifty years, the labours of scholarship have put into our hands an extensive magazine of texts, translations, expositions. We can hardly measure our debt to this work.

Yet it lies in the nature of the case that the more successful, masterly and profound the expositions, the less do they prepare the mind for the actual Oriental scene. For one who expounds a religion has first to conceive it—that is, he must penetrate behind surface variety to its central meaning, its "essence." The assumption is that each religion has its own unitary spirit or genius, and that the genial expositor will detect it. Yet the *prima facie* diversity and confusion, which it is the aim to resolve, remains an important part of the picture, especially when we attempt to judge those impending or possible relationships between religions with which our own study is concerned.

For it is just on their growing edges, often by way of the gropings of deviating groups, that living religions are likely to encounter one another in new relationships. What these religions in their main features are reputed to be, I can assume and shall assume as known. I shall attempt rather to bring before you some relevant aspects of the actual religions which current expositions do not make prominent.

Let me begin with a trait which at the outset baffles our efforts to segregate the populations of the East according to religion, namely, their capacity to belong to more than one religion at a time.

PLURAL BELONGING

To us of the West it is likely to be an outstanding puzzle how a man, if he is either clear-headed or honest, can distribute his devotions among two or more religions. If a Bulgar is converted to Islam does he not drop Christianity? If an Arab is converted to Christianity does he not drop Islam? We take it as one of the peculiar points of Chinese psychology that a good householder can be Confucianist in his daily habits and yet call on Taoist or Buddhist priests to conduct a funeral. Is this an amiable inconsequence, or is there a sounder instinct at work?

We cannot dispose of this difficulty by saying that Confucianism is after all not a religion but a system of ethics. Many Chinese will assert this, and with some pride in their natural humanism of outlook: "We Chinese are not religious: Confucius was a social pragmatist, agnostic about all metaphysical matters, and we follow him in this respect." Certainly, Confucius was interested chiefly in social and political reform; he was leaning against the superstition of his day. And he is as chary of committing himself on points of theology as Socrates; his evasions are frequently the purest pragmatism. He will not say that the spirits of the dead exist, nor will he deny their existence; but he advises treating them "as if they were present!"

Yet the reticence of Confucius always stops short of negation. He never denounces the main lines of the world-view of his time—Heaven and Earth, the divine creative pair, half physical to be sure, and half more-than-physical, and above them both a supreme inaccessible being, Shang Ti. He uses these terms colloquially; he quotes the old saying, "The good man is a ternion (third partner) with Heaven and Earth." So much might be taken as conventional acquiescence in common usage were it not for the fact that Confucius adds two important notes of his own:

He considered himself to have a personal commission from Tien (Heaven) to carry on his teaching. When he was attacked during his travels at the town of Kwang, he reassured his anxious followers with this remark: "Tien has appointed me to teach this doctrine, and until I have done so, what can the people of Kwang do to me?"* Then again, it was he who uttered one of the great religious sayings of all time: "He who offends the gods has no one to whom he can pray." For those who offend the gods, the cruder religious sense provides punishments; Confucius indicates instead the germane and inner consequence of sin, inability to make a sincere prayer!

Confucius was reticent about religion (and still more so about metaphysics); but he was far from being without it. He conceived righteousness and its spread as a cosmic demand.

* There are various versions of this story; the attitude it conveys appears to have been characteristic of Confucius, and to have come to expression on more than one occasion. Cf. Hattori, Unokichi, Confucius's Conviction of his Heavenly Mission, *Harvard Journal Asiatic Studies*, April 1936, p. 99.

We shall understand the position of Confucius better if we compare it with that of Lao Tze, the traditional founder of Taoism. In both of these men, metaphysical reticence is a dominant trait. Lao Tze was a mystic; and mysticism is reticence made a principle.

In Lao Tze's thought, there is one real being, the One for which the name Tien is itself too tangible: it may be referred to as "Tao," though this word is but a substitute for "the name which cannot be named."* "Tao" suggests to the mind an inner Order of the universe for which our terms "Reason" or "Law" or "Spirit" may not be too far astray; "Logos" has something the same meaning.† Tao is the source of all things; omnipotent by non-assertion. It cannot be said to appoint to men their individual tasks, for it is not personal; nevertheless by its simple existence it establishes a standard for human life, "Be thyself like Tao; achieve in thyself the same supreme simplicity, the non-assertive naturalness which is the most real of all powers." Thus Lao Tze like Confucius, but still more radically, was a simplifier of religion.

From this point, the two teachers diverge. Agreeing that Heaven issues no explicit instructions, Lao Tze infers that all concepts of virtue are artificial, self-conscious, and dangerous, whereas Confucius infers

---

* The word Tao is said to be untranslatable, but it is hard to see with what justification; for in so far as it is a sign for the unnamable, it is the precise equivalent of any other sign for the same thing! It is not "Tao" which is untranslatable, but the connotations lying in the Chinese history of the term.

† Dr. Karl Reichelt has discussed the relationship of these terms. See his *Truth and Tradition in Chinese Buddhism*, 163.

from the same premiss that we men must think out the code of righteousness for ourselves—the guide of life is to give things and actions their right names. Confucius saw the danger of externality in all codes, and issued a repeated call for sincerity; Lao Tze saw the same danger and *denounced the codes*—the consciousness of virtue is the beginning of unvirtue!

> "If one loses Tao, virtue appears;
> If one loses virtue, benevolence appears;
> If one loses benevolence, justice appears;
> If one loses justice, propriety appears;
> Propriety is the semblance of good faith
> And the beginning of disorder."*

In this sequence, the Confucian virtue of "Li," harshly translated as "propriety," occupied the lowest position. For Confucius, "Li" meant a sensitive appreciation of fitness: it was the inner discrimination, of which propriety would be one external expression. But it did lend itself to the abuse of formality on the part of any but a conscience of determined energy.

It was China's misfortune that, in presence of this divergence of judgment, it felt obliged to choose the one and reject the other. If it could have found a way to combine them, the resulting civilisation would have had that unexampled strength which could arise from a union of intuition and conceptual definiteness. But China, after some wavering, chose Confucius the clear rather than Lao Tze the obscure. It turned away from its most gifted speculative intellect; and the cult of Taoism, though enriched by the marvellous

* *Tao Teh King*, chapter 38; translated by Paul Carus, Open Court.

work of Chuang Tze, tended to an unrestrained and formless supernaturalism.

Meanwhile, what now concerns us is the common element in the Confucian and Taoist views of the world. For both, the human scene was related to an abiding, unknowable One. To the true Taoist, this One was an inner presence, an ever present guide-without-rule, the principle of absolute naturalness: "The great man is he who does not lose his child's heart." Chuang Tze tells of the butcher who for twenty years had no need to sharpen his knife; for, guided by Tao, it always found the joint! For the average Taoist, as for the average Confucianist, the One was intangible. The metaphysical bleakness of its image left it powerless to curb the superstitiousness of the popular mind. The springs of imagination and feeling were not reached by the highest elements of these reticent faiths.

In this circumstance we have, I believe, a clue to the welcome which China, in the first century of our era, gave to Buddhism.

Why Buddhism was so widely received in China is one of the great historical mysteries. On its face, Buddhism is in complete contrast to the temperament of China: with its dour estimate of human life, its other-worldliness or rather non-worldliness, its monastic establishments, how could it gain a hearing in a land of (alleged)* contented and natural humanism?

* Professor Roderick Scott points out that the Chinese character is by no means resumable in these reputed traits; the pessimistic Russian literature finds in China an extraordinary public; and Lu Shun whose note is, if possible, more despairing, is very popular.

In Hu Shih's judgment, it was and remains alien, a cultural calamity, a "sterile heritage."

The answer may be in part that Buddhism came with the prestige of distance, and was considered to represent at that time a higher civilisation. Its subtle logic, its capacity for uniting speculative flight with criticism, opened a new world of thought. Its scriptures had the air at once of authority and profundity. The men who brought it were impressive in their character and in their zeal to translate and expound. They used no pressure; they presented what to them was truth; they had no political interests; they seemed to open a new region of reflection.

We may say more than this: Buddhism offered a vaster sweep to the imagination. The Buddhist supermundane spaces and times were majestic and filled by the shapes of the growing Mahayana pantheon, the Buddhas, the Bodhisattvas, their divine attendants and messengers. This world of ordered majesty so far outshone the disorderly tumult of demonic shapes in the folklore of the symbolic characters of decadent popular Taoism that it could absorb the main figures and displace the rest. It became the inspiration of a new field of art.

If we think of all this as an imposing fallacy we may say of it, with Hu Shih, that "The Great Witch has swallowed the Little Witch": Buddhist superstition has engulfed the lesser superstition of China, and thereby the Chinese genius has assumed a voluntary slavery to a spirit which can never be its own. The simplicity and reticence of Confucius and Lao Tze are forgotten. The sensible Chinese habit gives way to an assumed pessimism and an emulation in ascetic excess: monks publicly burn themselves to death! Self-immolation, forbidding of widows to remarry, perhaps foot-binding, are among the cultural bequests of this foreign spiritual disease.

In this light we can read subsequent developments of Chinese Buddhism as a conquest of the conqueror by the invincible rectitude and humour of China. Not that Buddhism is persecuted or refuted—though these things occur—but that a thoroughly Chinese version is made of it. Bodhidharma in the sixth century had brought from India a form of Buddhist absolutism, the "Meditation Doctrine," teaching that the real is for thought "The Void." The discipline of this school consisted in the rebuke of intellect, its Buddhism in the dogma that there is no Buddha except one's self and that one's self is also a nothingness! This paradoxical teaching is China's opportunity: the spirit that could conceive Taoism with its precepts of Wu-wei (non-assertion) can find itself at home here. It becomes the Ch'an Buddhism (lineal ancestor of the Zen Buddhism of Japan) whose teaching is that there can be no teaching, and whose illumination must be private and silent. In this quietistic scheme the pretentious mansions of Mahayana are reduced to phantoms, and Buddhism itself to helpless indifference if not to absurdity. Thus, in Hu Shih's interpretation, the Chinese spirit wrestles with the invader and renders him impotent.

I admire the wit of this view of the career of Buddhism in China, but is it complete?

We can hardly say that the indefinable being of Buddhism has meant "nothing" to China or to Japan, when Zen is still one of the educational forces of the state. Buddhism has known that the world cannot be built upon a mere negation. Its "nothing" is like the modern flux-philosophy of "no-substance," a philosophy whose cult is not the atom but the event. An event is no-thing. Buddhism proposes that the absolute is spiritual law; and a law is not a thing. Yet a law is a positive sort of being, just as Tao though undefined gives one something to live by. And the notion of "law" has the advantage that it can concern itself imaginatively with cosmic history and with the destiny of human lives. It is a conception capable of bringing a moral order into the unrestrained fancies of supernature.

Allowing Buddhism this positive role, we see that there is no contradiction between it and Confucianism, but rather mutual completion. Confucianism is a minimal theism, leaving in its wake the hunger of unanswered questioning; its agnosticism was a standing call for a supplement. Buddhism gained its hold by supplying that want. The immensely renewed energy of art is a sufficient evidence that it brought to the Chinese spirit freedom rather than restraint. Its abuses are to be corrected, within its own frame. The neo-Confucianism of Chu Hsi and of Wang Yang Ming are, in fact, developments of Confucian metaphysics which are made possible by the long sway of Buddhistic metaphysics.*

* Hocking, "Chu Hsi's Theory of Knowledge," *Harvard Journal of Asiatic Studies*, April 1936, 119.

But on the other hand, Buddhism alone could never be a sufficient religion for China, because it lacks local and particular relation to Chinese culture. This Confucianism has. And while Confucianism in its classical form cannot suffice for the life of a modern China, something of it remains necessary: no other system can supply to modern China the indispensable continuity with its own past.

We see, then, why it is not alone natural but sound that a Chinese should be a Confucianist and also a Buddhist; the one performs the particular and local functions of religion, the other the universal and transcendent functions.* So long as no one religion does both, two religions are likely to be better than one.

Let me recapitulate what I conceive to be the substantial and permanent services of Buddhism to China.

1. Its speculative grasp. Though it carried the enigmatic doctrine of "the Void," yet in its imagery and thought it went far beyond this view: it was from the first a well-developed world-view.

2. Its depth of feeling. Here it responded to a patent need of the Chinese temper; it released the emotion which lurks behind the placid—sometimes stolid—Chinese facade. If there are any people in the world untouchable by religious feeling, the case for all religion—and especially for Christianity—is at once gone. The Chinese in any case are not such creatures. It was their own passion for which they found in Buddhism a more adequate measure

* I recognise that the actual picture is hardly as neat as this. There is likely to be a fringe of Taoist animism in the *ensemble*, and the pantheons mix.

both in art and in ritual. Buddhism has survived there the ages of persecution and neglect largely through the fact that the Chinese family-sense has found satisfaction in its rituals of mourning and marriage. The mark has no doubt been overshot; but the facts of history are unmistakable.

3. Its elements of negation. World-flight cannot make up a life-programme for China, nor for any other land. But there is a problem of evil which every mind must face as a common human problem; a religion which looks at fortune as a matter of particular divine favour, to be sought by divinatory gambling, is not a religion for a great and thoughtful race. An element of detachment from the world was needed to develop the soul of China; it is a part of any valid picture of human life; it is a condition for any firm and unfickle insertion in the world's serious business. I cannot agree that the "pessimistic" elements of Buddhism have been wholly alien to the Chinese spirit.

4. Religious democracy. The earlier Confucianism tended to confine the household worship to the minor deities and the cult of the ancestors. The Bodhisattvas of Buddhism were supposed to be concerned to bring the truth and the goods of religion to the common man; Kwan Yin, the goddess of mercy, who is represented in most homes in eastern China, stands for the direct concern of the highest in the lot of every man. This is but a strand of democracy; it does nothing to heal the breach which exists everywhere between the professionally religious and the mass of the people, but through giving the people a direct way to the most exalted powers it does something to render that breach supportable.

It may be asked why the same phenomenon does not take place with other localised religions. The answer is that it does. In Japan, Buddhism has supplemented Confucianism and Shinto very much as it has the Confucianism and Taoism of China. The relations of the several cults have sometimes been hostile; and sometimes a direct effort at amalgamation has occurred, as in Ryóbu Shinto. But the present *modus vivendi* allows life to all these, and the people have no difficulty in effecting their own transitions and divisions of religious labour.

In India, Hinduism as a local religion needs its supplement in a religion which is universal. It is capable of developing such a religion from its own resources, and in the Ramakrishna-Vivekananda version of Vedanta has done so. But it has another supplement! For among the most remarkable events in recent religious history is the return of Buddhism to India after a long period of relative exile. The opening (November 1931) of the new temple at Sarnath, on the site of the deer-park which was the traditional scene of Buddha's first sermon, was attended not alone by delegations of Buddhists, but by representatives of various Hindu societies. The leading address was made by Pandit Narendra Nath Das Gupta, head of the Sanscrit College of Calcutta. In it he declared that Christianity had shown itself a failure, in view of the inability of Christian nations to keep peace with one another; made a well-justified assertion that Buddhism had never spread itself by any political means nor by use of force; and then welcomed the advent of what he called the *Hindu-Buddhist civilisation* of India, which he prophesied was destined to become the spiritual canopy of Asia.

The possible amalgamation of Hinduism with Buddhist conceptions, and with Buddhist universality, would constitute another instance of the natural supplementation of the local and the universal in religion—so long as the fundamental dilemma is not solved. Dr. Das Gupta, on that occasion, seemed to feel no obstacle in conceiving himself as belonging to both religions.

2

RELATIVE FORMLESSNESS

THE word "organisation" is western; so is the fact and the talent. Tagore has an essay which indicates his justified dread of it. When we consider that China and India contain the oldest human societies which carry a continuous culture, we appreciate the marvel of the circumstance that this continuity is not effected by administration: Oriental institutions have been self-conserving. Families have carried on an education in customs, eked out by a highly informal, irregular and largely mnemonic oral instruction, which has sustained with astonishing fidelity the flavour of these civilisations through millennia. This is in general true of religion also.

The temples and mosques have no roster of members (I except modern Japan), no parish boundaries, no fixed incomes.

There is, apart from the structure of the great family, no widely recognised hierarchy of authority, with defined headship. The Lama of Tibet claims authority over all northern Buddhism, but the claim is a shadow. In India authority takes the vague shape of the caste ascendency of the Brahmins, devoid of centre. There are several "sankaracharyas," headships of important temples or groups of temples; but there is no chief priest, no council of cardinals. A good Moslem, remembering there was once a Califate, will mention to you the chief centres of wisdom for his faith—and of these Cairo will be first; but the others will stand in various orders, Damascus, Rihad, Baghdad, Tunis, Jerusalem—according to the bias of the speaker; and whether he will include Delhi, Lahore, Aligarh, Teheran, depends on his sect and his native land. Though there is now a lively interest in orthodoxy, there is no man and no group who can definitively pronounce what is orthodox in Hinduism, Islam, Buddhism, Confucianism.

Having no defined parish, the Buddhist priest has no parish duties. His offices are solely in his temple. The people who wish his services may go to him; he does not go to them. For the most part he does not know, or only vaguely knows, who they are.

He is responsible for the education of any youths who are accepted as candidates for the priesthood, but not for the religious education of the community (there are scattered exceptions to this rule, as in Burma).

There are numerous consequences of this formlessness. One is that no one knows how many Buddhists, Confucianists, Hindus, Moslems there are, except by assumptions about local populations. The usual statistical tables represent Buddhism as having 150 million adherents. But since there are some 250 million in China and some 50 million in Japan who are, as it were, part-time Buddhists this estimate is far from significant. Buddhism has somewhere between 150 million and 500 million adherents!

Where a new religion enters as a competitor, or a new religious movement begins to interfere with traditional religious habits, the incomes of temples will at once decline; but the priest, having no "flock" to whom he can address himself, and being unaccustomed to public preaching, can do little to meet the situation: he can only concentrate his fire upon the bearers of the new movement.

Chief of all, there grows up a mental gap between the instructed religious professionals and the laity, which no one is responsible for removing.

This leads to a third trait I wish to mention: the variety of human types within a religion, and of the ways in which these persons are attached to the religion.

3

VARIETY OF PERSONNEL

THE distinction between priest and people is a primitive distinction. In the Orient it runs especially deep because of that looseness of the tie of membership which we have just noted.

Partly because of this gap, there tend to spring up intermediate groups in which the Orient is peculiarly rich. There are the *lay mystics*—the dervishes, sadhus, sannyasis, yogins. And there are the scholars in religion—pundits, gurus, cadis, muftis, magistrates in the sacred law.

The priests and monks.—It is a general rule that a religion cannot be safely judged by its priests, a rule doubly important in the Orient. It is equally a rule that the priests, as the direct administrators of religion, will naturally occupy the foreground in an observer's picture of the religion, and will be likely to colour its repute more than any other class. With notable exceptions, they are the least edifying of its representatives: it is they who supply the chief instances of abuse for those whose interest is in abuses. If one seeks commercialism, ignorance, grossness, exploitation of human trouble and sentiment, they are to be found among the priests. There have been not a few Buddhist and Taoist priests in old China who were justly enough characterized as "engaged in a funeral racket". They deal largely with a low variety of magic. One cannot look save with mingled horror and pity at the type of medicine dispensed in the typical oriental temple.

> There you may see such scenes as this: a woman whose child is sick kneeling before an image, pronouncing sentences of prayer and shaking a box containing bamboo sticks. One end of the box has an aperture, and at last one of the sticks is shaken from the box: it bears a mark; this mark is the indication to the attendant priest which remedy is prescribed by the god. The sacred medicine there dispensed is commonly accompanied by the injunction that it is not to be taken on the premises of the temple.

The monk, though he may serve a temple, is as a rule, a person of different quality and temperament. He is necessarily a man of studies and of books, as the priest, who commonly enters his calling by apprentice-ship, need not be. One sometimes passes directly from a public temple to a monastery enclosure (as at Amoy) and finds himself in a different world. In the temple, the traffic with credulity; in the monastery, a library well stocked with books, modern and ancient, with the sciences as well as theology—an atmosphere of thought, a search for enlightenment, not unmixed with distaste for the doings of the adjoining temple. In the order of the monkish life there is everywhere an invitation to the physical laziness, and to the moral laziness of routine. The reforming monk, Tai H'su, has set him-self to combat this tendency, and by stimulating activities of public teaching and writing, to renew the initiative of thinking so that Chinese Buddhism may be prepared to meet the questions which the contemporary world is putting to all religion. Where such responsibility is felt, one finds among this group perhaps the finest examples of the spirit of Oriental religion.

The lay mystics.—Turning to the intermediate groups, the *lay devotees*, especially numerous in India, present externally a somewhat motley and extravagant aspect of the religions, and at the same time a certain original and experimental trait. They represent religion escaping convention and routine. They may be individuals or groups, occupying some such position to the religious establishment as the "Oxford Group" among Christian sects.

The order of life traditional in India invites the man who has been in due order student and householder to become in later life a recluse and then a sannyasi. Having renounced all ties with the world, the caste man, instructed in the Vedas, may wander about as a teacher of those who have need of him. The non-caste-man may give himself over to pilgrimages to sacred places, making a specialty of some bit of austerity which he displays—eked out perhaps by some trick of entertainment—for which he expects to receive alms. These non-caste or low-caste mystics, the "sadhus", do obtain contributions from those who are ready to admire the exhibition of piety, as also from those who fear the resentment of a man having magical powers if the hoped-for gift is refused. But the extent of the livelihood thus provided clearly depends on the state of faith in the general public; and it is one of the favourable portents of the religious horizon of India that their number has been diminishing of late, through the necessity of earning an honest living.

Distinct from these travelling sadhus, are the *yogins* (or yogis), usually persons of fixed abode, engaged in the active practice of religious discipline for the sake of self-mastery and ultimate release through enlightenment—perhaps also for the sake of the enjoyment of those supernatural powers which are promised to the adepts in the yoga. Some of these men are of notable power and character; some of them have gained a remarkable control of physical and mental processes, a control of which the true yogin never makes public display. Their art deserves, and is receiving, the attention of western scholars, less however for its religious meaning than for its psychological and educational value.

While this group as a whole has little to contribute to our knowledge of the significance of the religions they profess, they show—as do the dervish orders in the Moslem world—the *widespread impulse which animates the laity of Asia and northern Africa to take a step out of religious inertia and receptiveness,* and to seek through such means as are available to them a more immediate awareness of the divine. From the confusion of their experimental gropings there arise from time to time mystics, poets, local prophets with messages for their environment.

The scholars.—The group of pundits, once a compact learned class in India and China, and a powerful body of authority in the Moslem world, is now everywhere touched by the unsettlements of thought, so that the rigorous thinker tends to be untypical. Just on this account, while he is historian, jurist, authoritative interpreter, he is also an important guide to the possibilities of growth.

There are, of course, the scholars whose interest is in the conserving of tradition, the knowers of the

Vedas or of the Classics, the men in whose memory lies intact, line for line, the whole of some source-book or of some commentary not anywhere to be found in writing. But there are also the scholars who have added western training to their own learning, and who remaining within the frame of the Asiatic religion are chiefly concerned with an improved interpretation. They have read our philosophers and our men of letters; they have worked out their own theories of the relationship of eastern and western thought; they are prepared to say what their sacred books ought to mean—which is undoubtedly what they do mean. Sir Sarvapali Radhakrishnan, himself a distinguished member of this group, quite rightly admonished me not to seek the "growing points of Hinduism" among the sadhus and sannyasis, but rather among the scholars who had received the discipline of science. I judge that we require both to take the full gamut of the living religion. The true sannyasi, in whom glows the ancient fire without the disturbing winds of modernity, must be taken together with the modern scholar and his clarified (presumably over-intellectualised) conceptions of meaning, to constitute an adequate picture.

The people.—In all of the above we have been taking for granted the largest and weightiest of the groups, the masses, from whom in the long run all support of the religious specialists must come. Of the religion of the people, there are three things to be said:

(1) Their religion is more alike, the world over, than are the religions to which they belong. This is due in part to the neglect of their education of which

we have spoken—the mental gulf between the instructed priests or monks, and the uninstructed com-
moners, peasants, artisans, whose religion takes the
form of the lore of family and neighbourhood. The
people know little of the theologies professed by the
specialists. They may not so much as know the name
of their own religion; for to them, it is not "Hinduism"
nor "Shinto," it is simply religion, or perhaps simply
tradition, for they know no other. Their observances
vary not alone from religion to religion but from
valley to valley. There is the maximum difference in
ritual and folklore, but the maximum likeness in ideas,
the underlying conceptions and the attitudes are everywhere the same.

(2) This religion is everywhere superstitious, and
utilitarian. It is pervaded by a gambling temper, fear-
some, gullible, servile, and exploited. This is not
peculiar to Asiatic religions; for superstition of the
same type is rife also among the Christian peasantries
of Europe.

> A sacred book is a thing to work magic with, whether
> it be the Li Ki, the Koran, or the Bible. "Cutting the
> Koran" is a ceremony quite the equivalent of opening the
> Bible at random for guidance. After the appropriate pre-
> liminaries one is to open the book where the fingers enter,
> read the first sentence or part of sentence on the page,
> and then guess how these words apply to the business in
> hand.*

Superstition is not a peculiarity of any religion: it
is a function of the stage of enlightenment, and especially of the degree of training in scientific thought

* B. A. Donaldson, *Moslem World*, July 1937, 245 ff.

which a population may have received, and beneath this, of their capacity for such training.

Among the more primitive peoples of Asia and Africa there are likely to appear waves of religious excitement taking forms of exaltation or fanaticism or frenzy, at the summons of some wizard, enthusiast, or prophet who may be wise or merely mad, an ambitious Mahdi or simply a shrewd rascal with some scheme of profit in his eye. There are travelling agitators who appear among distant Moslem villages telling the people in the name of true religion that they must give up liquor, stop dancing and singing, put their women into purdah, and above all stop eating chickens or pigs; in brief, take on numerous new taboos from which they have been free—while the loose animals now worthless to them are driven to market by hands strangely ready for the work. In this ubiquitous union of credulity and craft lie the universal seeds of revolt against all religion.

(3) The religion of the people *has a sound kernel*. The universal sense of the presence of God, and the intuition of the direction in which the will of God lies, comes often to evidence among them. It is seldom that the crust of superstition and dehumanising fear or corruption becomes so fixed that a glow of genuine religious life does not live beneath it.

A typical instance: a story told me by a prominent Japanese Christian of his mother, a Shintoist. He was born the eighth child of a poor farmer north of the mountains; at his birth his mother was in despair, not for means to feed him, but because she saw no way to provide for his education and career. In her distress she betook herself to a neighbouring Shinto shrine and made a vow to the deity: if this deity would take her son under protection, she would eat no eggs henceforth as long as she lived. This was a severer hardship than the words at once convey; for meat was an almost unknown luxury in that household, and the sea was remote, so that eggs were the chief source of protein food.

When the boy was old enough to leave home he was taken by an uncle to the city, where at last he found employment in a printer's shop. He became skilled in that trade. He was converted to Christianity. He used to spend time after his day's work in setting up short and simple explanations of Bible texts; for the explanations of the foreign missionaries were difficult for the Japanese. He put Christianity into the common idiom. There grew up a demand for these explanations, the young man found himself prosperous. The time came when he could leave his work and make a visit to his home. He found his mother in poor health. He said to her, "Mother, you should now terminate your vow; you are losing your strength; for your sake and mine I beg you to return to your right diet. I am now established in life; the vow is no longer necessary. Further, I have learned a new religion, which shows me that this vow has no validity. You are released from it." His mother replied, "My son, no one ever outgrows the need for God's care. I made my vow for life, and I shall adhere to it during my life."

This tale was told with a touch of pride which showed me that the speaker felt in his mother's piety a hold on God deeper than his own had been at that moment.

It is among the people in every land that one finds the souls in which awareness of the divine is least overlaid. And it is among them that directness of speech is most usual. Reference of experience to the divine power, and direct address to God as "Thou," come naturally to their lips. Much of the poetry of Tagore is a new rendering of such folk-poetry as is found in the working people or the wandering singers of Bengal. This is one of the songs, sung by boatmen on one of the wide rivers of East Bengal, as reported by Professor K. Mohan Sen, a rare and noble spirit, who has wandered afield and collected many such from the singers themselves:*

> I am a lamp on the water; at what ghat did'st Thou place
> me on the stream? Where is the ghat at which Thou
> sett'st me afloat?
> In the dark night speaks but the garland of the waves, and
> under it ever flows the stream like a flowing, deep
> dark night;
> My only companion is the little flame, and no bank and
> no end is near . . .
> O Ocean, in which all rivers find their destination,
> Friend, End of all endless movement, how many bends of
> the river are still before me?
> And Thou, with what call wilt Thou reveal Thyself to me?
> Thou wilt take me from the water, and there, under the
> protection of Thy arm, near to Thy heart, wilt
> extinguish the burning of the whole long journey.

To find a similar directness of the consciousness of God in our own tradition, we should have to look to men like Augustine or Anselm, who write their diaries or conduct their philosophies as a dialogue with God. What is a deliberate form in such writers is the staple

* This version is abbreviated: what is given is approximately that published by Arnold Baké from Professor Sen's original. The reference of the poem is to a custom of women of Bengal. On special occasions they place lights in shells on the streams, together with their names; and then from their boats taking them at random from the water, read omens in the names and in the manner of the light's extinction.

of life among many of the common folk of Asia. It is because of this soundness of substance that the lay mystics, of whom we have spoken, emerge in such numbers from their ranks.

As science filters through into the general consciousness of Asia, the superstitious elements tend to drop away like dead leaves. The religious impulse is likely to drop off with them. But the conditions from which religion arises do not drop away; they remain ready to reassert themselves.

4

THE PLACE OF THOUGHT
AND DOCTRINE

ONE of the most striking traits of the Far Eastern religions as distinct from those of the Near East is their reflective character. The religions of China are at the same time philosophies. From the time of the Upanishads, the Indian scriptures move in the atmosphere of thought and argument.

In Buddhism, at the foundation, there is an appeal to the moral experience of man. Recall the "Noble Fourfold Truth": (1) the truth about suffering—we are asked to observe and to generalise to the effect that life and suffering are inseparable; (2) the truth of the cause of suffering—we are asked to follow a close analysis which shows the root of suffering to lie in the craving for separate individual existence; (3) the truth of the cure of suffering—a clear deduction from the diagnosis, this craving must be extinguished; (4) the truth of the way to effect the cure—an adjustment of means to end, resulting in the "Noble Eightfold Path." I doubt whether this diagnosis and way of cure are final; all I am here concerned to point out is the method of address to the hearer. Never, I suppose, has a religion set out its case with so complete an appeal to human rational powers and empirical judgment.

This reflective element is not the only element in

these scriptures. All sacred books claim to be inspired, and in most cases to be revealed; in accord with this idea of origin-from-beyond their style is likely to be oracular, aphoristic, dogmatic. The books of India and China are not lacking in these qualities; only, the invitation to reflection is there also. Even in the epics, poetry and speculative thought are mingled; and the Bhagavadgita is at once a song and a flight of metaphysical argument.

The temper of the books is reflected in the attitude of the adherents: reason so far from being rejected because of its human limitations is welcomed, taken for granted as pertinent to the great objects of the faith. Even in the language of prayer, there is mirrored the elevation of thought. Note the universal Hindu prayer:

> "From unreality, lead me to Reality,
> From darkness, lead me unto Light,
> From death, lead me to Immortality."*

These religions are reflective.

This is not true of the scriptures of the Semitic religions. They never resort to argument, nor establish doctrine on human experience. They are built of history, poetry, aphorism, prophecy, exhortation, dogma, command. They appeal to faith, that is, to recognition, intuitive insight, the voluntary leap of trust in the prophetic speaker, surrender to the divine will (conveyed in the word "Islam") as represented by the human medium. In this sense, all Semitic

* Brihadaranyaka Upanishad I, iii, 28.

scriptures are Islamic, including Judaism and a portion of Christianity.

There are some who consider this atmosphere of dogma and command an ultimate advantage, as appropriate to the manner of revelation, an address of God to man admitting no reasoning on the part of the creature. It is in this sense that Dr. Kraemer's principle of classification* stigmatises the religions of the farther East as based on naturalism and human effort rather than on supernaturalism and divine grace. For my part I confess that it is just the honouring of thought and of human effort as a factor—never the whole—of religion which in the religions of India and China bring me a sense of freedom and self-respect, as if the use of reason were not a religious misdemeanour. I never enter the realm of Buddhist literature without feeling that certain traditional fetters and browbeatings have dropped away.

One result of this difference is that the Christian minister and missionary are frequently less equipped than they should be to meet the serious thinkers of the Orient on their own ground. In conversation with the Hindu pundit or the Buddhist monk, the Christian missionary, as a rule, moves in a lesser world of thought; and there is substance in the contention that Buddhism is better fitted than Christianity for interpreting the modern world, so far as that world is one of rationally apprehended law.

* Kraemer, Hendrik, *The Christian Message in a Non-Christian World*, ch. v, pp. 142 ff.

At the same time, in the Orient thought is never identified with religion. It is secondary.

It is important only as an auxiliary to salvation. In contrast to the West, there is no independent cult of metaphysics. In the Vedanta, the purest leap of Eastern speculation, to be saved requires knowledge, but conceptual apprehension is not enough; the term "realisation" indicates the difference; one must *enact* the truth in one's own immediate being; one must have a true metaphysics because the way of release involves realisation. With us, in the opening of the modern era, metaphysics divorces itself from direct responsibility for showing the way of life: Descartes writes philosophy as a science, not an ethic. This independent metaphysics may easily run off into a conscientiously unapplied play of reason; our students of metaphysics do not as a rule consider that they are occupied with their personal salvation. In the East, the subordination of metaphysics preserves it from triviality. Prabhu Dutt Shastri puts the matter thus:

> "To us, a philosopher is not a dialectician . . . but one who hungers after spiritual insight, who is ever trying to reflect his knowledge and beliefs in his life and deeds . . . who tries to penetrate to the core of reality . . . not much affected by pleasure and pain and leading a life of purity and love. . . ."

Thus thought, we may say, is in the Oriental religions both honoured and humiliated. It is respected, not snubbed as extraneous to faith. But it is not flattered, as if it were identical with faith, and as if man could be saved by knowledge. Religious thought is an instrument of religious practice.*

Accordingly, the identity of a religion lies not in any terms of doctrine, but in its sources and its goal. The good Hindu is he who, taking the Vedas as guide and text for his social and meditative life, aims at the salvation of release in conscious union with Brahman; given these, his theory of the world may be what it will.

On this ground we begin to understand the astonishing acquiescence of Hinduism in doctrinal difference. Christianity splits into sects because it believes in the possibility and necessity of a true formulation of creed (should we put this into the past tense?). Hinduism has at least six systems of philosophy, thoroughly incompatible with one another, and all of them orthodox! Logically speaking, a system it regards as a "construction"; and since an element of human artefact enters into it, together with its intuitive truth, there may be alternative constructions having the same religious value. The symbol of entrance into the

---

* Almost, one might say that religious truth is taken pragmatically—any creed is true if it leads to salvation ! But not quite : for if the meaning of the creed were solely its result, that lively interest in reaching true doctrine would hardly survive. What we can say is that there is a pragmatic test for the retaining of an hypothesis; if it leads to religious achievement, it is not to be excluded, even though it may be a leaky vessel.

In the religion of the people there is a thoroughly crass pragmatism; and this is embedded in the *ipsissima verba* of the Puranas, the popular scriptures of modern Hinduism. Perusal of a very little of this massive literature will convince the reader that the Hindu is not by his religion weaned away from interest in worldly goods : he is promised by it liberal blessings in both worlds.

Buddhist brotherhood is not the recital of a creed but the performance of an act:

> "I take refuge in the Buddha,
> I take refuge in the Rule,
> I take refuge in the Order."

There are limits to toleration even in Hinduism, but they are not drawn by philosophy nor doctrine. Buddhism, in its earlier days, could not be tolerated— not because it had a different world-view—but because it separated itself from the Vedas, denounced the element of caste in religion, altered the code of social behaviour, and delared the Vedanta Sadhana a failure on pragmatic grounds. "Neither does indulgence nor the orthodox asceticism *bring emancipation from suffering*; there must therefore be another, a middle path." And even where there can be no co-operation, the Hindu will continue to show respect for whatever intuition has revealed, and the human attitude of reverence has held sacred.*

* So Sir S. Radhakrishnan: "What the soul of man holds or has held sacred must remain an object of respect even when we differ from his theory about it. . . . My religious sense does not allow me to speak a rash or profane word of anything which the soul of man has held sacred. This attitude of respect for all creeds, this elementary good manners in matters of spirit, is bred in the marrow of one's bones by the Hindu tradition. . . . The true teacher helps us to deepen our insight, not alter our view."

5

CERTAIN INFERENCES
IMMUNITY TO DISPROOF

FROM the four characteristics of Oriental religions which we have just reviewed there are conclusions to be drawn which bear upon our interest in a world faith. One is that we are not likely to dispose of any of these religions by showing it to be in error: an Oriental religion is extraordinarily hard to refute!

It is not that the standard of truth and falsity fails to apply to the dogmas of religion. It is that a religion cannot in general be identified with a doctrinal position. It is easy to assign to a religion a definite position, and then show that position mistaken: most religions have had the experience of being refuted in this way. The reply is always in principle the same: "That is not our position." And the point is, this reply is always permissible!

For no religion, Oriental or other, can be identified with a metaphysical position; nor can the issues between them be stated in such terms. This follows at once from the subordinate role of the metaphysical element. It is hard to reckon the amount of heart-burning and friction which a recognition of this truth might have spared.

Take, for example, the experience of *Advaita Vedanta*, often refuted by western scholars, philosophers, and missionaries; perhaps the oftenest refuted of any Oriental school of thought.

Advaita (non-twoness) is presumably the purest monism still professed among men: there is but one real being, one knower, one witness, one self; this One is absolute, untouched by any breath of plurality, hence separate from all finite existence, from all finite selves in their distinct and personal being. The true being of the human self is solely its identity with Paramatman, the One Self. Of the One we may think, from our human point of view, as Sat, Chid, Ananda— Being, Knowing, Bliss: in itself it is without qualities. The refutation of this position lies in the consideration that if the One is the only real, this world with which our experience starts cannot be real, and we who start with it cannot, in our personal separateness be real. We ascend to the real by a path of negation: "This is not real, that is not real." But if Advaita is to be taken literally, this path is not real and our reasonings are not real, and the result, the negation of non-reals, is mere emptiness. If now we could regard Advaita Vedanta as the "central core" of Hinduism,* we might regard Hinduism as substantially disposed of.

But in spite of the complete agreement of the chorus of western critics of Advaita from Hegel to Royce, Macnicol, Schweitzer, where are the converts? Were they perhaps somewhat immunised by the refutations already present within the Vedanta tradition itself?

* Cf. Nicol Macnicol, *Is Christianity Unique*, p. 31.

A common diagnosis, based presumably on a felt spiritual climate, which is undoubtedly critical of the reality of visible and separate things; an emphatic racial intuition, the primary thesis of all spiritual truth.

For Ramanuja had already set up a Vedanta of "unity in difference" (Visishtadvaita), and Madhva a Vedanta of duality (Dvaita); and since they based themselves on alternative interpretations of Upanishadic texts,* these critics-from-within remain good Hindus and good Vedantists. And the Advaitists of to-day simply say to all such critics, "This pure nothingness of the visible world is not precisely what we mean"; behind this rejoinder we cannot go. Dr. Macnicol observes them sadly: "Through the centuries, many Indians who are intellectually travellers by the Advaita road, try at the same time as men of religion to hold on to the reality of both God and man, being convinced that something deeper than reason demands this."† They remain, in his view, better as men than as thinkers. But even if those thoughts were abandoned as fallacious, they need not—as we have seen—leave Vedanta to correct them. The refutation of a doctrine does not refute a religion.

The same principle shows the ineffectiveness of any attempt to deal with the oriental religions by placing them in *an evolutionary or dialectical order*, as Hegel did, thus subjecting each in turn to the gentle fate of being superseded by the next higher member of the series, after having enjoyed the moment of validity in superseding the earlier version of truth. In this respect, I surmise that most western students of Oriental religions are Hegelians at heart, tending to

* Cf. S. C. Sen, *Mystic Philosophy of Upanishads*, p. 76 ff.
† *Is Christianity Unique?* p. 32.

conceive the religions as members in a rational series whose terminus is necessarily one's own view.

It will, therefore, be well to consider the method of Hegel with some care. It was his belief that the several stages of civilisation were characterised each one by an Idea, the prevalent conception of the Real; and that this Idea expressed itself in all phases of the civilisation, its art, its institutions, its political type, its religion. Religion was in fact the most germane and direct expression of the spirit of the civilisation; it was the distillate, so to speak, of its characteristic attitude towards the world. Now Hegel's conception of history is based on his belief that the succession of civilisations is fundamentally a succession of these ideas of the Real, or of God; that there is an element of necessity in the series of stages through which the conception of God passes; and that he, Hegel, could discern these stages in the confused procession of world history, beginning with China, and moving westward through the Asiatic world.

It is easy, in the light of our fuller knowledge, to criticise the characterisations which Hegel gave of the great religions. It is more rewarding to glean from them their multitudes of penetrating observations; and to learn, in particular, how well Hegel could corroborate in detail the general unity of meaning between a religion and the other aspects of a concrete civilisation. He saw, as few philosophers have seen, the necessity that religion be particular, as a whole culture is particular.*

* An appended note to this chapter will give an example of the present value of Hegel's work, p. 133.

But however genial Hegel's insight into the several religions, it remains true that the very notion of a serial order among the great religions is mistaken; that it is, in fact, *inconsistent with the dialectical principle itself*. For no people and no religion ceases to think. If Chinese religion, for example, is defective, it will be Chinese experience which will discover it, and the cure should come in China, not in India. Why must the movement of fundamental racial thought pass from region to region, as if thought were no longer productive in its old haunts? If Indian religion is defective, why must the more perfect stage emerge in Tibet?

In point of fact, India has never ceased to think. Buddhism as a dialectical criticism of Brahmanism was a product of the Indian spirit. Buddhism itself is still typically Indian: its yoga, its karma, its nirvana, its negative life-sense are all Indian. There were indeed new notions which arose on Tibetan soil. But the elements in northern Buddhism which have most widely influenced Asia, the typical Mahayana, were presumably also products of later Indian thought.

Neither has China ceased to think. It has shown less power than India to perceive *how* contrasting truths which supplement one another can unite in a "synthesis." But it has kept the elements, either as the two parties of Confucianism and Taoism, or as the uneasy amalgam of Buddhism with the other faiths. Neo-Confucianism in the twelfth and fourteenth centuries was, as we have seen, an approach to a true synthesis. And to-day Confucian thought has taken a new grasp of the problems of contemporary China and bids fair to mark another stage in its dialectical journey.

Hegel's view of the passage of the Idea from place to place has, to be sure, a certain empirical justification. For it is true that fresh blood, new geographical conditions, political disturbances, stir mankind to new assemblages of culture. It is also true that mere persistence in thinking does not ensure that the process of thought will move on. Agitation is not necessarily progress. Whether any new proposal is an advance or a retreat or a helpless wallowing about in insignificant variants is not certified by the mere fact that thought has gone into it. There is no advance without new energy and new insight. But given these conditions, the dialectical principle must assert itself, and better *in situ* than in a new sphere where continuity is lost.

The principle is, that *from any position partially false there is a nisus toward a truer position.* Hence no imperfect position is ever one of stable mental equilibrium even when it is guarded by an implacable orthodoxy or invincible spiritual somnolence, or the momentum of a world of acquired habits. Living thought and living religion never stand still. The "dialectic" is incessant and everywhere.

And this being true, the next stage in any dialectical movement is the natural property of the possessors of the previous stage. It can only define itself as that which these previous ones have always dimly known as their more perfect meaning! Then it follows that no imperfect position can be fastened upon any religion as its true definition. Or to put the same principle in positive form:

> The better stage of truth is on the line of march of each religion, and can rightly be claimed by each religion as its own.

This principle indicates the essential difficulty of placing religions which are still alive in dialectical or other serial order, with respect to metaphysical truth. Such truth, like scientific truth, is potentially everyman's property.* Hence the religions assigned to positions lower down on the scale will simply reject the assignment. Dead religions are the only ones that will submit to serve as stepping stones to our own evolution!

On the same principle we see the *futility of fixed doctrinal definitions* for living religions. Religions must have creeds; and nothing is more natural than to identify them by means of their creeds—"Islam is the religion of Allah; and Allah is the one and only God conceived as a transcendent being of absolute power." A creed which is erroneous or defective shows in the most striking way the need for con-

---

* There is another kind of truth in religion to which this dialectical principle does not apply, namely, truth about particulars. "I believe that Allah is God alone, and that Mohammed is his prophet"; the process of self-criticising thought might be allowed to bring men everywhere to the truth of the unity of the deity; but that kind of thinking would not alone bring them to the particular prophet. If God has offered to men a specific revelation, or specific channel of revelation, such truth would have to be accepted as factual, and beyond the reach of human reflection on purely human experience. We note the radical importance for our problem of the claim of this type of truth; it will be discussed in Chapter IV.

version. This mode of appeal requires for its effectiveness two things: that the adherent of the religion in question agree to the defectiveness of the creed or article; and that he accepts it, at the same time, as having been his own. All experience shows the rarity of the conjunction of these two conditions. A characterisation of defective belief which strikes home will either be disowned, or else will become an *agent of change* within the frame of the religion criticised.

This point is of such practical importance that I shall ask your indulgence in giving a number of illustrations.

A missionary in the Near East has perforce to decide for himself in what respect the Moslem conception of God differs from the Christian conception. Some have reached this formula: the Moslem God is a God of power; the Christian God is a God of love.

This is not an arbitrary delimitation. That being to whom absolute and unquestioning submission is due, and whose ways are past finding out, is from our human point of view a power over us. The name Islam may be fairly rendered "submission," "surrender," an attitude proper to the "Wholly Other" and the All-powerful. But let this antithesis be preached or published (as it has been), and it immediately becomes an agency for bringing forward in Islam an assertion of the elements of love that are in Allah. It is pointed out that the Surahs of the Koran open regularly with the phrase, "In the name of Allah, the merciful and compassionate," and that these dispositions are aspects of love. The dominant attribute of God in the Koran is *Rabb*. He is "the Lord"; but the meaning of "the Lord" is not alone all-powerful Creator and Sustainer, but also Bringer-to-perfection of his creatures. The Koran does not use Ab (Abba), fearing the anthropomorphic strain in the idea of "Father"; its notion of "Nurturing-toward-perfection" is its preferred variant of the same spirit of tenderness. This tenderness is further emphasised in the attributes next in order of prominence in the Koran, Rahman and Rahim, kindness and mercy. And by the next, according to which Allah is Al-Ghaffar, the Forgiving: "If ye would love God, then follow me, and God will love you and forgive your sins, for God is forgiving and merciful" (Surah 3, 30). So long as the debate is based on the texts, it tends to lose itself in the shades of meaning of words. But if a Moslem in his personal experience finds his God all-loving as well as all-just and all-powerful, and has thus through the way of Islam arrived at what the Christian regards as truth about God, how can the Christian deny him the right to that development within his own religion? And this has been true of many a Moslem mystic. What words in any religion are more poignant than these from Al Hallaj:

> The voice from Heaven crying in the night
> "My soul is weary of my lonely throne;
> Unloved is he who owns the world alone
> In sole, supreme and solitary might.
> One crowning wonder yet remains to do.
> Behold, I make this mean and crumbling clod
> The loved and lover of Almighty God,
> Almighty in power, almighty in loving too!

> Behold, I call my creature, even thee,
> The poor, the frail, the sinful, and the sad,
> And with my glory I will make thee glad:
> Come unto me, my friend, come unto me."
> E'en so, the voice from heaven I heard, and came,
> And veiled my face, and plunged into the flame.*

It is true that Al Hallaj was crucified for blasphemy. Not, however, because he made God "almighty in loving," but because he appeared to identify himself with the divine freedom and might. Some notion of the love of God lies in the line of development of any mysticism; and mysticism is common coin of all the great religions.

The Christian protagonist need not and does not halt his argument at this point. He points out that the word love is ambiguous; and that the love of Christianity is qualitatively different from that of the Moslem mystic. This is not a matter of detail: nothing is more disastrous to religion than a misinterpretation in its name of love. Christianity itself has historically exemplified this danger, through falsely indulgent or sentimentally tinged notions of a benevolent deity; every human weakness echoes itself in its conception of love, and likewise every human strength. If one were to succeed, then, in marking off the Christian conception of the divine love from the Moslem conception by a definite conceptual boundary, Moslem thinkers would still be left with the question whether the Christian conception is better or truer; and if so, whether, in turn, it cannot be found within their own natural line of march.

* As translated by the late Sir Cecil Spring-Rice.

A striking illustration of this principle—no meta-physical boundaries—is to be found in the common Christian judgment that Allah is a *distant God*. The saintly, learned, and much beloved missionary to India, Dr. Nicol Macnicol, treats this judgment somewhat as an axiom in his Wilde Lectures.* Having encountered Islam first in the Near East, and in the person of Moslems to whom Allah appeared a remarkably near companion, I thought at first that this must be an inadvertence; but as I continued, I saw that it was taken as a clear inference from the Islamic doctrine of God's transcendence: Allah is beyond reach, beyond thought, and rejects all mixture with the world, as by begetting or "incarnation" in either the Hindu or the Christian sense. The logic of the matter seems clear even when one remembers that violent word of Mohammed, "Allah is nearer to you than the great vein of your neck," until one considers the paradox of remoteness. No two can be so near to each other as two who are *both withdrawn from the world*; and indeed how, except by such withdrawal, can nearness be attained? If God is transcendent precisely in the sense in which the believer's self may be said to be transcendent, God's remoteness from *things* may be the primary condition of his nearness to the believer. This appears to be the actual inference of Moslem faith; for to the good Moslem, God is surely a near and present God, more so, I am tempted to say, than to most Christians.

But suppose this tendency on the part of a living

* *Is Christianity Unique?* p. 36.

religion to claim as its own whatever is held superior in another is pushed to the point of contradiction? Instances of this are not lacking; they occur in any period of rapid growth. I am tempted to cite here, as introducing apparent inconsistency with traditional views, the notable work of the late Sir Mohammed Iqbal. In his *Six Lectures on Reconstruction in Islam* he draws widely upon the resources of recent European philosophy for interpreting Islam. In the developing idea of God, Sir Mohammed finds Bergson's conception of the *élan vital*, as the single creative power of the changing world, most germane to the meaning of Allah. It requires no deep discernment to discover profound antitheses between the immanent *élan* and the transcendent Allah. But suppose these antitheses to be accepted! Are there to be no mysteries for human thought in the idea of the deity? When the word "antithesis" is substituted for the word "contradiction," western thought should begin to feel at home! It will not do to complain of as "contradiction" in another religion what we accept as "antithesis" in our own, or even honour under the resounding title of "dialectical theology!"*

I choose these illustrations from Islam because, in general, Islam is ready to define itself sharply, not alone to accept contrasts, but to make its own con-

---

* Professor Widgery, in his excellent review of Dr. Macnicol's book has pointed out that the paradox whereby a religion of minute divine predestination still makes strong appeal to human freedom—a paradox presented both by Islam and by the religions of Karma in a different guise— has not been absent from Christianity. He judges that it "could even be maintained that Hinduism and Buddhism give freedom a wider role than Christianity does."

trasts, and stand by them. If, then, Islam sets up any claim of ownership in the field of thought or doctrine, that claim cannot be attributed to indiscriminacy or lack of definitive character in religious temper. It becomes one of the data with which we have to reckon; and if the newly-accepted mark happens to be one which we have regarded as a differentia of Christianity, that differentia simply has to be abandoned.

This is true even when the differentia in question happens to be the *traditional intransigeance* itself. When the rector magnificus of Al Azhar, Sheikh Mustapha Al Maraghi, recently took part in the conference in London of the World Fellowship of Faiths, it was not alone the more conservative of his co-religionists who stood aghast. There were Christians in high places who felt that the rector had taken a step inconsistent with the character of Islam and were disturbed as by something which, rendering Islam more a part of the currents of the world's thought, ought not to be: "A growing Islam, a co-operative Islam, is no longer Islam." The Moslem position has been supposed to be that Islam is the only true religion. When, therefore, the rector refers in his speech to the "charitable spirit" of Islam toward all religions, not even limiting this charity to the "religions of the Book"; when he gives a full account of the common and valid elements of all creeds; and when in concluding he says to the Fellowship of Faiths that "the noble objective at which you aim is not contrary to the general principles of Islam," he is presumably taking a new step, and is most certainly acting as a man of courage. I judge that he had already determined that there was support within tradition for his action. But even if he had not thought this; if he had considered that a brittle and isolated Islam, losing its young people, was a waning faith, and that if a consistent Islam must be a dead Islam, it was high time to be inconsistent—he would have been wholly right, I believe, in regarding himself a better Moslem for his departure.

An illustration from the experience of India:

We have already referred to the general temper of Indian religion, sometimes identified with *Advaita Vedanta*. It has for over a century been the habit of western expositors to dwell on the negative attitude of Indian religion toward the present world, its bitter estimate of this existence as something to be escaped, its absence of motivation for positive social effort. As a general descriptive contrast of tempers between India and the West, or between India and China, there has been a degree of truth in it. But India has for a long time been aware of these descriptions which (except by Schopenhauer) were intended as criticisms. And being aware of them, it denies them any final validity. It points to the fact that there are many varieties of yoga including the yoga of work, of discipline, of energy (Saktiyoga); that popular Hinduism and its scriptures are as little world-rejecting as the Vedas themselves; and at the same time, *it begins to be otherwise*. It begins to heave away from the philosophy of Maya, and from a passive social attitude. It brings into the foreground the latent incentives to action which are available in its own literature. The Ramakrishna movement and the Arya Samaj distinguish themselves by initiative in education, and philanthropy and social reform. Among other vigorous spirits, Professor Benoy Sarkar makes himself exponent of an Indian Positivism; and has these things to say of the Hinduism of the immediate future:

> "Hinduism has acquired a new lease of life under the auspices of the Ramakrishna-Vivekananda socio-spiritual Gestalt," which, with its social activities, will "constitute the living religion of India in the twentieth century."

> "Hinduism has ever been the religion of charaiveti (marching on) and digvijaya (world conquest), of dynamism and progress, as proclaimed in the Aitareya Brahmana (vii, 15; viii, 1, 39). In Hinduism is to be found the cult of power, activity, and manhood. The purusha (man) of the Atharva Veda (xii, 1, 54) declares his ambitions to the earth as follows:

>> " 'Mighty am I, Superior by name, upon earth;
>> Conquering am I, all conquering,
>> Completely conquering every region.' "

Dr. Sarkar cites also the Upanishads, Vedanta literature, Gita, Puranas and Tantras as preaching the gospel of strength, showing that it has never been absent from the sources; Ramakrishna and Vivekananda have but revived what has been there, and have extracted from the Upanishads alone "strength enough to invigorate the whole world."

What Vivekananda finds, Dr. Sarkar formulates in three propositions, whose order I venture to transpose as follows:

(1) The fundamental equation, Jiva (man) = Shiva (God). Whence, service to man is service to God.

(2) This carries with it a demand for self-respect and courage, enabling the individual "to combat diffidence,

overpower the thousand and one frailties of human existence" in himself—a message of special importance for the submerged and repressed groups.

(3) It carries also an assurance of the power of soul (Satyagraha) in external affairs. It is the soul or spirit which is the instrument for demolishing or transforming the untoward conditions of the surrounding world. This is the concrete freedom of personality.

By Positivism, Dr. Sarkar means an insistence on "worldly duties" as a part of the ethical requirement. He finds in Vivekananda a "synthesis of the positive and the idealistic."*

Dr. Macnicol is right in feeling that India is in these developments swerving from its traditional—its medieval—character. He describes Vivekananda and Radhakrishnan as "seeking to reinterpret Hinduism in a sense that will make moral struggle and effort a reality" and comments that "to accomplish this the whole system requires transformation." He feels that the departure involved is so great that the identity of the system is threatened: "If Christianity were only true to itself, it could transform the world; unless Hinduism is splendidly untrue to itself, as one must hope it will be, its world will remain to the end unredeemed."† These words, "as one must hope it will be," are to be recorded to the honour of a great soul, a Scottish Mahatma—for they recognise what it is hardest for an aggressive Christian to acknowledge, that even such changes will not require that Hinduism cease to be Hinduism.

* *Ramakrishna-Vivekananda and the Religion of Progress.* International Bengal Institute.
† *Is Christianity Unique?*, p. 52.

The conclusion of all this is not that metaphysical thought should cease, as impertinent to the problem of world religion. Just the reverse. The persistence of such thinking is inevitable; and is showing itself one of the most powerful agencies for bringing the minds of men into agreement. Only, it *makes for the assimilation of religions, not for conversion of all the rest to one of them*, as alone true or as most true. It has no tendency to diminish the number of extant particular religions.

With other literature, the philosophical literature of the world is now the possession of all the major languages; appropriation takes place wherever there is the appetite for that phase of truth. As a common body of thought, it aids in leading the minds within all religions toward a common goal. Because of this appropriation, no existing religion will be displaced, solely as being permanently identified with an untenable doctrine. The more abominable of the tenets of the religions, the various hells, torments, demons, are shuffled off by a silent process of oblivion, well known to Christians in the history of their own demonology and hell-lore. As general enlightenment quietly buries the superstitions, so it alters the emphasis on all traditional dogmas, and relegates some of them to the ash-heap. The religions, thus released live on, perhaps with renewed vitality.

It will doubtless be refreshing to metaphysicians to contemplate themselves in the unaccustomed role of agents of agreement among men! Yet this is what is clearly happening, as the persuasive and pertinent elements of modern thought make their way into the fabric of all the religions. But let us hasten to say that this effect is relatively slow and impersonal. It is only as philosophy ceases to be an individual opinionation promulgated with personal or party insistence that this greater influence becomes perceptible. Philosophising makes sects, whether within or without religion; but when it becomes the atmosphere of a civilisation or an age, it extinguishes quietly the grosser errors and ushers men with equal silence towards a common mind.

6

CERTAIN INFERENCES
PLASTICITY TO CHANGE

A SECOND consequence of the characteristics above mentioned is that these religions can bend and alter without breaking. Their relative formlessness and deficiency in organisation, together with their capacity just now dwelt on for absorbing new ideas into their structure, tends to enable them to survive when by most signs they should be ready to perish.

Polytheism itself contributes to their elasticity. For polytheism allows the several god-figures to wax and wane in general esteem, as men's thought and feeling changes; and the less worthy of them to be relegated to Limbo, as their functions cease to be sought. Hinduism is, in general, too retentive for its own good; much of its strangeness to western eyes is due to the conserving of ancient observances; modern Hinduism selects and discards, lightens its ballast, and becomes more viable. So Chinese and Japanese Buddhism choose among the rich gallery of Bodhisattvas. If the East, in respect to its religions, were as rigid and unchangeable as it has been reputed, the impact of modern life might have swept the existing religions away.

There are many who feel that some, perhaps all, of the now-living religions of Asia are in fact on the way to death. I refer now not to the strong anti-religious element of Asia in whose eyes all religion is moribund, but chiefly to Christian observers who judge this of non-Christian religions. Thus Professor Duncan B. Macdonald writing in the *Moslem World* in 1932 says: "The West is imposing its whole materialistic mechanised civilisation upon the East. The East knows it, resents it, but is defenceless. Its own culture, its own religious and philosophical systems of thought and conduct, are falling like card houses. Its young men, trained in Western thought in the modern secularised schools, are losing all religious feeling. Their own religions cannot stand the strain, and nothing is being put in their place." As long ago as 1908 the Schaff-Herzog writer said of Buddhism that it "has passed into a hopeless and senile decay."

I have no doubt that the extreme stress which the social and political changes in Asia are imposing on the religious systems finds them in many ways un-prepared to resist; and that their hold on the youth of Asia is weakening even more conspicuously than that of Christianity on its youth. The swath of non-religious or anti-religious sentiment in Asia will, I judge, be very wide. But I cannot agree that the existing religions are moribund or likely to disappear. Islam is expanding not only in Africa but in Japan, China, India, Germany, and even in England. The figure of 220 million Moslems commonly given should probably be, at present, between 240 and 260 million. The number of printing presses in the Moslem world was 200 in 1900 and in 1935 was 880. Hinduism and Buddhism have shown unsuspected capacities for new leadership, especially among the laity.

I do not discount the gravity of the picture in Asia. Let me therefore offer a hasty sketch of the conditions which the religions there have to meet, and of their resources for meeting them.

The agencies of change which are sweeping over all Asiatic culture are of two sorts. There is a wide receptiveness to what, for lack of a better name, we may call "modernity." And there is a forced draft of change, actuated by self-conscious political forces, nationalist in their main inspiration. These forces have been acting slowly for a hundred years; but now they move under the spur of acute political fear and hope, realising that a new Asia is being made and that time is of the essence of the outcome for every people. It lies in the nature of the situation that these two agencies support one another. This will appear if we analyse for a moment the meaning of that vague term "modernity."

Modernity, as it appears in Asia, means four things:

(1) The acceptance of *science and technology* as necessitating, in any world-view, the inclusion of nature as through and through a realm of law and not of magical accident.

(2) The will to effect social change *by human efforts*, not to suffer passively nor to rely on the divine powers; and to do this by *ad hoc* association, not through the inherited social forms.

(3) The resulting enhanced *importance of the nation* as the chief instrument of self-conscious social change, replacing the "divine will" as an agent of those major

social shiftings which are beyond individual or family control.

(4) The *pragmatic ultimatum* issued to all sentiments including the religious sentiments, to defend their existence by their results, estimated in realistic terms.

In the effort to meet these forces, the mental life of slow-thinking masses has been spurred everywhere beyond its power of effective functioning. It is reacting emotionally more than it is thinking; it is groping for stable centres of prestige; its religious inclinations become for the moment the plaything of its more immediate leadership. If a Gandhi is at the centre of confidence, Hinduism will be strengthened, even while undergoing in two decades more revolutionary change than in a thousand years before. If a Jawaharlal Nehru is at the helm, then, while there will be in India no such wholesale relegation of religion to the background as in Turkey, all religion—Hinduism and Islam, Sikhism and Christianity alike—will retreat in interest.

But where is the leadership which is prepared to deal on its merits with the religious issues, or with the more radical question which the shadow of Russia makes acute whether all religion is not a worship of the unverifiable and unmeaning, and so a source of stupefaction rather than of power. In all Asia, there are few priests competent to meet this question in concrete and convincing terms.

Can the intellectual leaders do better? The scholarship of Asia, prewarned by what knowledge it has gained of western history, is attempting the task, and brings much competence to it. There are several new journals of opinion strongly edited. In India this scholarship is for the most part conservative in the literal sense of the term; holding to a Hinduism or an Islam firmly rooted in the historic sources even while radically reshaped. In China, it is divided between conserving and discarding; but under the spirited and courageous initiative of Hu Shih, its tendency is to cut away from the past, and gather together the ingredients of a new civilisation—free from religion—on a naturalistic and humanist basis.

Hu Shih was a student under John Dewey; and the younger leaders have in the main followed suit. Nevertheless, in China as in India, there is a group of scholars who continue to identify themselves with local religion, and who essay reinterpretation of Confucianism or Buddhism.

But there is not enough competent thinking in Asia to-day, nor enough translation of this thinking into popular language, to reach the minds or affect the suffrages of the restless masses. It is evident that the old religious leadership realises the gravity of its own situation, and the life-and-death issue which confronts its systems as a whole. They can rely for a generation on the momentum of custom, and the sturdy rootage of ancient rites. But they are driven to an unaccustomed activity of thought, under a spur of danger which is not wholly an auspicious spur. And it is natural that they should everywhere *split into two widely divergent parties*; the radical reversionists, and the radical reformists—those who see the one hope in recovered orthodoxy, and those who see the one hope in a courageous acceptance of the new, so far as it can be united with a much simplified faith. It is fortunate perhaps that they hardly realise—nor do we—the danger to Asia and to the world if all the ancient ideologies of faith should disintegrate rapidly and with them the ethical framework of life for a half of all humanity.

As Professor Stanley Cook has recently pointed out, the contact and clash of cultures, instead of being a stimulus, can also be a solvent of civilisations. The broadening of political unities and the intermixtures of systems of thought which occurred over the Near Eastern area, from the sixth century B.C. onward, contributed not a little to the collapse of ancient civilisation.

The question is whether the rate of production and assimilation of new thought can at all keep pace with the rate of destruction of the old. It is hard to believe that the Oriental peasant of to-day is better able to hold his moral balance during this transformation than the citizen of ancient Rome. He must find some sort of stability in the institutional roof over his head —some source of the conviction which his own experience is not generating for him. The ancient systems have but a sorry shelter to offer, for they are being mechanically disturbed rather than convinced. They are not leading, but are being led; they are forced into new moulds before they can realise what those moulds signify. They do not know from within which way to go; hence they go the way which at the moment seems to have the greatest prestige, or to exert the greatest pressure.

As a natural result of the prevailing unreadiness, we find everywhere in Asia, not alone the disintegration of old patterns, but a fever which is at least a sign of life—improvisation, producing moral half-way houses as emergency constructions. There are numerous artificial and incongruous amalgamations of ideas, destined to have a short day, and to melt into other forms. Let me mention some of these:

The influence of science.—It is not surprising that in the Orient as in the West the word "science," even where it is but vaguely understood, should act as a fetish. The most reactionary of the religious groups realise that this new power is not transitory; "science" is something which all the schools must teach! All the schools accordingly hang out the new flag. Among the masses science intrudes itself not in its spirit but in its applications, medical and technical: the machine, which no one escapes, brings the machine-using mind, which is on its way—often reluctantly—to become the machine-making mind. In the greater universities on religious foundations, the Hindu University at Benares, the Moslem University at Aligarh, science is well represented; in Al Azhar, there is at least a place for it. The fire is lighted and in time it will burn.

But what does science say to religion? What does it reject, and what assert? Is the yoga "scientific?" and if so, is the scientific aspect of it the significant thing about it? Does science reject the gods? Does it reject God? Hinduism and Buddhism can make good claims to be in accord with the spirit of law in the world, for is not the law of karma the basis of all earthly happening? And Tai H'su, the reforming

Buddhist monk, cries up the atheistic aspect of Buddhism, declaring that it of all religions is most in tune with science because it is founded on law and rejects the notion of a personal deity.

But the science thus warmly adopted will prove a barren bedfellow for these special hopes. For the law of karma is no law of natural causation: it is moral and metaphysical, discriminating the ethical qualities of action as no causal law can do. The law of karma is, after all, a form of the old "final cause" from whose intrusions modern science had first to clear its house. The alliance is artificial; and the attempt to trim any religion to the outline of a scientific world-view, while curing much superstition, would be likely to leave that religion shorn of its *raison d'être*.

The influence of social activism.—Human self-help by self-conscious analysis of social situations and the rational application of remedy—this is the most searching of modern novelties in its effect on public discussion, and the religions hasten to give evidence that this attitude is within the spirit of their sources. But the change is deep-going, and it *falls hardest on the local religions*; for they are identified with the existing social structure, they are its sanction and its apology.

Hence the reformer and the priest are usually different persons. They can hardly take the same pace. The reformer finds little inspiration for his work in the council of the religious authorities or in the scriptures. The editorial policy of the Indian Social Reformer has been to consider each reform on its own merits, independent of tradition; and to seek the approval of the religious authorities afterward. There is one Gandhi who finds in his religion the principles of social change; for most others the tie to religion appears subsequent if not hampering.

And reciprocally, for the religions the tie to social changes is unhappy and uncertain. Hinduism cannot, for example, give itself wholeheartedly to a utilitarian treatment of its cattle while still holding that its moral contribution to the world lies in the doctrine of ahimsa, "harmlessness" toward man and beast, with unwillingness to kill. Gandhi, with characteristic courage, takes upon himself the onus of putting a sick calf out of its misery: the great step is taken, a beginning is made. But the next steps are distressingly slow. There is a Liberal Hinduism which claims the sanction of religion for the following causes: rural uplift, non-violence, anti-untouchability, economic justice, political activism, democracy. Assuming that we know what economic justice and democracy can be in India, the programme is representative. But the Liberal Hinduism group is not attempting to speak for Hinduism as a whole. Nor can any group so speak on any formulated social programme.

Islam has the severest struggle to face in view of the social revolution now sweeping the Near East. For Islam, while a universal religion, is also a local religion in our sense, namely, that the Koran is a book of law and custom prescribed with much detail. And it is a book which has guarded itself against alteration with peculiar stringency. Yet the Near East is the seat of a new national life, involving new legislation on social themes. The young men who are mapping out these legislative programmes are likely to retain their allegiance to Islam, partly in conscious contrast to the course taken by Turkey, partly because they find in Islam the spiritual expression of their national life. These legislators thus face a peculiar dilemma. They will shape their new codes largely on European models. They will retain the Koran. Then the Koran must be reinterpreted; its spirit must replace its letter. In this transition, the religion will follow rather than lead, its relation to the new societies will be anything but simple and unambiguous. The coming half-hour will be no easy one for religion or for state.

The influence of nationalism.—National patriotism enlists a type of idealism which is independent of any religion; yet having a religious quality, it reaches out for the alliance and sanction of such religious groups as exist. The religious bodies feel the demand. It is a political demand; but it is also a demand which comes from the nature of religion itself to be organic with whatever idealism is active in the world. It was a Chinese Christian who said to me with grim bewilderment, "The idealism of China is outside the churches"; he could take no satisfaction in the freedom of the churches from that agitation. All religion feels the criticism of abstraction from the "real" religiousness of the time. Yet to absorb national patriotism is equally an embarrassment.

The local religions yield most readily to this pressure. They are already immersed in the corporate life of the people; they are flattered as they find themselves acquiring a new value, that of a national badge and asset. Hinduism feels justified in regarding itself as the spirit of India, tries to qualify for that role, even asserting a spiritual unity with Islam in the national ethos. Confucianism is little able to speak for itself, being less an entity than an ingrained attitude of a people; yet it tends under the national stress to become an entity, wins new definitions and new thought, and tries to speak for the spirit of the eternal China.

It is the *universal religions which chiefly suffer* under the new national invitation: they are placed before the harsh alternative of accepting in each place the national cause as their own and so undergoing internal division and shame, or of inviting persecution, perhaps extinction. In Japan, the religions have all been required to avow allegiance to the national cause. Buddhism in Japan has for some time fully accepted this function; certain of the sects of this most pacific of religions, notably Nichiren and Zen, have prided themselves on developing warriors and statesmen for the service of the state. Nichiren, since its inception, has been an ardent exponent of patriotism. And even Kwannon, the goddess of mercy, has been conscripted to service as patroness of the continental campaign.

The situation is characterised by an absence of clear thinking on both sides. The nationalists do not see that the cosmic demand and approval cannot be taken by violence, nor made a useful auxiliary of the foreign office; and while the local religions most easily find themselves at home in such a role, they are most liable to be corrupted by it. On the other hand, the internationalists frequently fail to see that religion has its

local responsibility to the state; it must make citizens
capable of criticising the state; it must also make citizens capable of giving themselves to the state in every
just enterprise. In point of fact, the universal religions
do yield in such situations, Buddhism and Christianity
alike; they yield because they are not sure of themselves. And the result is an uneasy amalgam of a
national sentiment dogged with a consciousness of
having prostituted what must be free, with a religious
sentiment cursed with an inner self-reproach for suc-
cumbing to expediency.

In this hasty review of the difficulties which are
facing the Oriental religions and their meagre resources
for dealing with them, I have not minimised the
dangers. Let me now repeat my conviction that these
religions are *not on the way to death*. This judgment is
based partly on the visible vitality which shows itself
in the new versions of Islam, Hinduism, Buddhism,
largely of lay origin, which continue to appear. Partly
on the vigorous self-consciousness of the scholars and
religious leaders in restating what to them is the
essence of their faith, each such restatement being
in fact a union of ancient truth and modern understanding. But chiefly on the fact that the primary
sources of the several religions are not in these more
vocal quarters, but in longstanding habits of thought
and feeling which cannot easily be destroyed, and
which are capable of a *generalised* expression as well as
a specific one.

There is such a thing, for example, as a spirit of
Indian religion apart from the rites; and this spirit,

disturbed in its customary ways of expression, will devise and is devising others which are still of its own type. In Almora, on the slopes of the Himalayas, there is a hospital—a modern hospital though a small one, in charge of a skilled Indian surgeon. The hospital has a good name in the region; its facilities are always over-required. A year or two ago, a simple announcement appeared on its door: the surgeon was to be absent during a month for meditation and the practise of yoga; the work would be carried on by the staff. For our interest, the notable thing was not so much this leave-taking on the part of this Europe-trained head of the hospital as the complete understanding with which his absence for that purpose was accepted by his patients and the community. It was accepted as of course that the need to meditate should for him also take precedence of every other duty.

This may be taken as a symbol of the continued life of the old within the frame of the new outlook. They are not inconsistent in principle, and will find their own *modus vivendi*, largely through just such spontaneous reshapings of the central source of feeling.

It would, indeed, be absurd to suppose that "modernism" is about to impose its unrestricted stamp upon Asia. For modernism, while it has its intuitions, is not a magazine of results, but a group of unsolved problems. Such problems as these:

How to combine the scientific spirit with the free

moral life of man; how to combine secular initiative and pragmatic judgment in social ethics with a tenable detachment and otherworldliness; how to combine the visible inequalities of the naturalistic human being with the invisible equalities implied in any democratic code; how to combine the local and patriotic with the universal element in religion; and therewith, how to bring the church and the state into a relation of mutual help which shall be at the same time a free relation of mutual respect.

These problems sound strangely like problems with which we of the West are familiar, and to which we can hardly offer final solutions. The older religions may be a stage less prepared to meet them, but they are also less obsessed with modernity as a panacea. They are gaining the courage of their deeper convictions as against both the modernity and the religion of the West. Anesaki has to say that "There is increasing resistance in the East against the cultural pressure from Europe and America. . . . Asiatic culture was too strong to be entirely suppressed or eradicated. This resistance is backed by the awakening to the spiritual heritage, some phases of which would not admit a wholesale acceptance of scientific culture in its present form."* The Orient has not lost the eyesight by which, in detecting the weak places in our armour, it recovers its own sources of power.

If any religion were prepared with a set of answers for the questions which modernity is, that religion would indeed be in a strong position to attract the suffrages of mankind. Until this is the case it would

* Professor Masaharu Anesaki, in *Modern Review*, June 1937, p. 617.

surely be a tragic mistake if Christianity, on the assumption that it is fully at home with modernity and in harmony with it, were to push for the demolition of the old structures, or prematurely declare them dead.

NOTE ON HEGEL'S TREATMENT
OF HINDUISM

A glimpse of Hegel's treatment of Hinduism and Buddhism would show that his perception was juster in essential points, even a hundred years ago, than that of most present-day critics. He did not, for example, make the mistake of identifying the spirit of Hinduism with that of Advaita Vedanta. He did not interpret the Absolute of Hinduism as containing no principle to account for the multiform shapes of the empirical world. He did not accuse the religious spirit of Asia of being content with a disparaging conception of the place of man in the cosmos, as part of the play of illusion or of the deity's caprice. And even in his account of Buddhism, strange as that account seems to us to-day, he did at least recognise in that religion a positive contribution of great moment to the sense of human dignity, in its peculiar notion of the incarnation of the Buddha.

Hegel characterises the religions of Asia in general as religions of *substance*. He means by this that the Absolute Being is the sole and self-sufficient real, undisturbed, eternal, beyond time; whereas the many things including humanity and history are in relation to it mere nothings —dependent attributes of which it need not itself be aware. Despotic politics are a mirror of this notion of the Real. There is a point of grandeur in the Universe—one point only; and man is elevated by this grandeur. It is surely better to be subject in a world in which *one* is great, than to be the same abject creature with *none* great! This is the truth which makes the first high civilisation possible —that nobility in any spot, in some one spot, can be shared by all members of the same social body. The question of justice to individuals does not arise, because the enjoyment of a visible grandeur is vicarious. This is the secret of the long-contentedness of Asia in a centralised magnificence.

In India, Hegel proposes, this absolute substance is conceived as abstract unity—not as Heaven, not as Tao. A spiritual ultimate replaces the semi-material ultimate of China. This abstract One is not identified by Hegel with the vanishing point of being, as in Advaita. A principle exists whereby the many can be seen to *emerge* from the one. This is found in the Hindu Trinity, the Trimurti. But still, what emerges is inferior in reality to the One; it has no absolute importance; there is no dependence of God on the plural universe; it has beauty and immensity, but they do not restrain the profusion of being; the ugly, horrible, grotesque may also run riot. Man's own existence, caught in the wheel of rebirth, is fatefully involved in this caprice, contemptible and sad. Spirit, in Hegel's terms, has proceeded out of itself, but can find in this revelry of shapes no "return to itself": the energy of being is wasted in meaningless extravagance. Hinduism is the "religion of imagination."

Now, Hegel suggests, the thing that remains rankling and unfulfilled in this view is the unsatisfactory position of the human being; there is the necessity of elevating the dignity of the scene of his existence. And this is to be achieved by divine participation in it. This new stage he discovers in Buddhism, in the Buddhism of Tibet, where the Lama, the divine being present in the world, does at least confer an exaltation upon the actual in which he moves. The notion of the "return of Spirit to itself" through becoming aware of its own being and history is foreshadowed in this conception.

No one to-day would choose this language to express the spirit of these religions, nor the relations between them. But on this account, it is quite easy, in the vast tumble of Hegelian conceptions, to lose from sight its elements of profound penetration.

For example, Hegel's recognition that the characteristic side of the Hindu doctrine of God is not to be found in the formula "abstract unity" alone, but in a genetic relation between this unity and the "Trimurti" of esoteric Hinduism, saves him from the common blunder of calling Indian religion a pure negation of the world. I think he is right, too, in attributing to the Hindu view of the impulse which creates nature a certain uncontrolled and Protean abundance, like that of fertile imagination.

When he notes the element of the ugly and grotesque in the Hindu god-world, he shows his instinct for what is significant. He fails, to be sure, to see *what it signifies*. It is not that the Hindu imagination revels in these aspects of the world by preference. It is rather a perception that the divine *must deal* with evil, pain, suffering, terror: unless it does this, it is not carrying the burden of human fate. If torment is in the world, the Hindu must find the divine in torment; if destruction is there, he must find the divine in destruction—the god Siva in one of his many roles is his answer. This is the concreteness which Hinduism shows on the side of feeling, though less cogently on the side of intellect. The art of India is rendered heavy by the bodily incorporation of the evil element; at the same time it evinces a strong perception of the function of art, to make the adverse emotions understandable as part of a divine scheme. Art which insists on being ostensibly beautiful is less responsible. And so is that religion which sees God only in ostensible beauty. It is, I think, greatly to the credit of Hegel's perceptiveness that he raised the question about this aspect of Hinduism, though he lacked the data for an answer.

LECTURE III
WAYS TO A WORLD FAITH

WAYS TO A WORLD FAITH

THE present moment of history is not one of conspicuous harmony; but its very disorder sharpens the
point of the search for agreed principle, and its loss
of anchorage facilitates because it requires new
course-making. All religions are subject alike to the
belligerent wash of modernity; and all are silently
moved by the slow convergences of speculative thought.

Since the minds of men by all these ways are being
wafted toward a community of outlook, why not leave
the growth of a world faith to the kindly offices of
time? *Laissez faire* seems a promising policy; the more
so since the majority of mankind are disposed to
adopt it.

The chief difficulty with this comfortable proposal
is that the differences between religions are important.
A process which has no tendency to resolve these
differences can be no satisfaction to those who take
seriously the great enterprise of abolishing barriers
to human understanding. So long as we have at least
three religions whose faith, in its nature, rejects the
notion of a local boundary, there is latent conflict. If
the world is to come to rest with an accepted Buddhist
province, Christian province, Moslem province, each
of these religions must undergo internal change as
well. For each, at present, defines itself in terms of
world-wide acceptance.*

---

* Buddha's instructions to the missioners of his gospel refer not explicitly
to the world, but to an indefinite "many"; but like the instructions of Jesus,

Further, the differences, as we pointed out, are not solely disagreements on points of general truth or of general world-view; they include also questions of particular fact. Men like Hegel are delighted when they find that India has a trinity and an incarnation; they say, if these are true ideas, India has struck into the truth. But the common sense of piety is less than satisfied with such generalities. The question for common sense is not whether India has discerned the principle of trinity; the question is also whether this Trinity is truly thought of as Brahma, Vishnu and Siva, rather than as Father, Son and Spirit! No doubt common sense is here guilty of a stupid literalism, in a region where all conceptions are symbolic. True; but we must not fall into the complementary folly of supposing that only the general is to be considered, or that all religion can be dissolved into Truth. For the devotion of a religion runs toward *the specific channel* through which it realizes the truth; its books, its founders, its peculiar Words of God. It feels itself entrusted with these; and as trustee it is under responsibility to make this channel available to all men. The issues become issues of revelation, its meaning and historical arrival. This is the point upon which men like Dr. Kraemer draw their lines of distinction

it is the typical human individual, without regard to place, which they have in mind. I quote the version of those instructions given by Pandit Kosambi, formerly of the Benares Hindu University:

"Go ye monks in all directions, for the sake of many, for the happiness of many. Do not go two together;

"Your special house is at the foot of a tree;

"Your food depends altogether upon alms;

"Your clothes, rags collected from the bazaar or burning grounds;

"When sick, use mirabolon . . . it is the best purgative."

between religions. They not only admit, they assert, that among the religions there is, in general ideas, an "amazing amount of concurrence"; and that when we speak of "values," we shall find these impalpable things everywhere: but the issue of "truth" remains, and the issue of truth here means the very (biblical?) realistic and simple question, Did God speak specifically to mankind through Jesus as he did not speak through any other? Did God speak through Mohammed? Did God speak through Buddha at all—since Buddha himself never made such claim, but rejected the idea of a God who speaks?

Whatever the ground of the missionary impulse it is there, this aggressive conscience, which is restless until it conveys its particular gospel. Whether it is mistaken in its zeal, we have to enquire; the seeds of rivalry among faiths will remain as long as it persists. If it is over-responsible, *laissez faire* is under-responsible. Those who try to bring mankind to their own specific way of seeing God will always incur the reproach of the broad for their narrowness, the ridicule of the worldly wise for their lack of humour, and the angry rebuke of disturbed statesmen to whom they are at best intrusive busybodies. Yet the work they have done bears the nearest trait of disinterested good will that the world affords; and its fruits, direct and incidental, have left marks on history of which mankind will ever think with reverence as well as gratitude, and which would have been possible to no other conceivable motive. It is not quite credible that the ideology which has inspired these efforts is wholly mistaken: even if Christ were a pure myth, it is something that some men have tried to be like their idea of Christ, and something to be kept. It is also not quite credible that it is free from human defect.

We turn therefore to those ways towards a world faith which imply a positive effort to establish a concrete religion for mankind, not a mere group of true ideas and correct cosmic sentiments.

The first and most natural of these is the way of the primitive mission, the "way of radical displacement."

I

THE WAY OF RADICAL DISPLACEMENT

IT is the way of thorough: be done with the old allegiance and take on the new one. Recognise that when
the better way appears, the old way—whatever it
may have meant—is now for you a false way. It is a
case of either-or; you must decide; and to decide is
to act with a surgical decisiveness, "Come out, and
be separate." This summons is addressed to individuals. For the other faith as a system it implies an
aim at elimination.*

This is the natural method of the missionary consciousness; and under certain presuppositions, a logical
and necessary method. If we presuppose (1) that there
is a special revelation, an explicit word of God to
certain persons; (2) that this word reveals what could
never otherwise be known, a particular act of God's
will announcing a plan of salvation, which is therefore
the only way to be saved; (3) that the alternative is
eternal punishment or eternal death for all those who

* Dr. Robert E. Speer, writing in *The Moslem World*, April 1939, quotes
the following programme with the comment that "Christianity must
unswervingly hold this ground."
"Christianity proposes to win men away from the other religions by
bringing them something better, and to take the place of the other religions
in the world. . . . The attitude is not one of compromise but one of conflict
and of conquest. It proposes to displace the other religions. . . . The intention to conquer is characteristic of the Gospel. . . . It cannot conquer
except in love, but in love it intends to conquer. It means to fill the world."
The programme is that of Dr. J. A. Clarke in *A Study of Christian Missions*.

do not take this way; and (4) that God has referred to us as human messengers the task of warning mankind of its danger and of its one way of escape—thus shifting to our shoulders partial responsibility for the damnation of all who are damned from now on—then, for those who accept this responsibility there is but one thing to do.

I present the case with a deliberate baldness; because most of those who to-day insist on this Radical Displacement are inclined to blur one or another part of its necessary foundation. If we hesitate on any one of these four points, this method at once becomes dubious. We shall deal with these presuppositions. But first, let us note the great advantages of this method, and its achievements.

It is the original way of the modern mission. It has, in the main, built the Church in Asia; it has developed the heroic characters who have continued that Church in the face of incredible obstacles.

> We know the spirit of this method, and its Biblical authorisation. We recall the language of "The Great Commission"; the phrase of John's Gospel, "No man cometh unto the Father but by me," and that more specific phrase, "none other name."
>
> The spell of these words is far greater than their historical validity—which may always be questioned. If they were not the words of Jesus or of apostles, they were all the more certainly the convictions of the early Church. And they state an imperative which continues to be renewed in the experience of many a believer. The positive form of that experience is simply, "I have by him come to the Father." From this to the exclusive form, "There is no other way," is a long step, but a natural one; which may

be expressed as follows: "If this be true, then nothing which differs from it can be true. There can be no other, no second, no possibly competing or inconsistent word of God. The great things of the world do not duplicate themselves; truth does not split its stream. If then I can say, 'Here is truth,' I can say it for all men."

Karl Barth gives this position a characteristically vehement expression. The missionary, he says, is servant not of men but of the word of God. "The divine grace is to be announced as a miracle, not as a bridge that one may build, not as a sublimation of the natural"; hence the missionary is not "to fraternise, nor accept the fellowship of fallen faiths . . . in no circumstances is he to howl with the wolves."*

This policy is rigorous, and has aspects of severity, but this does not alter its necessity on the premises stated. And it has great advantages, both in pedagogy, and in emotional economy. It has the pedagogical advantage of single-minded simplicity of programme. It creates an intelligible issue, and calls out all the energies of the will.

Beside this advantage for the preacher, it has an advantage also for the convert: it understands the temper of conversion. If a new leaf is to be turned over, let it be a clean turn. As for the old way, one prefers not to be reminded of it; the effort to salvage remnants of what one now repudiates is not alone petty economy, it is repugnant to the meaning of a moral new departure. A new step in religion is not the formation of one new habit, but of many; there is a new set of practices to be learned, a new membership to be accepted, a new way of feeling about the world

* Quoted by Nicol Macnicol, *British Weekly*, London, March 30, 1933.

to be established. There must be rather a widening than a narrowing of the gulf between the new self and the former self until the balance is secure.

> I have referred above to Dr. Kraemer's mission in Bali,* to his desire to conserve what was characteristic in the harmonious native culture. The obstacles to carrying out this conserving part of the plan came from the Balinese themselves. To them, a religion is a way of doing things, of conducting the rites of marriage, the funeral, the celebration of birth, the seasonal feasts, the course of life. To be a Christian and to retain Balinese customs thus became a contradiction in terms.
>
> But there were concrete objections to a radical abandonment of old usages. These were urged by Dr. Kraemer; to omit them all meant to fail in carrying out the part of the convert in the total labour of the community, to become bad citizens. On the other hand, as the converts replied, to take part in these functions meant at every point an acknowledgment of the old gods and the old ideas. Continuity, even partial continuity, was in their view a compromise. They desired a clean breach.

We have to count upon a capacity in human nature for deviation. Man is a creature of habit; but he is also a creature who breaks habits: he has an impulse for moral as for physical exploration. Every youth coming to maturity finds two strong drives contending in him; the drive to be like his ancestors, and the drive to be thoroughly different. There may be, I think, impulses of cultural *Wanderlust* that seize whole groups and peoples, ripening them for group conversion.

And while we deplore the loss involved in all dis-

* Above, p. 47.

continuity, such loss is better than stagnation. Moral growth like the growth of a modern city must accept great waste—destruction of costly and usable buildings to construct better ones; it must admit its interims of acute suffering. The soft sensitivity which cannot endure losses and farewells for the sake of better things can have no place in the stern business of establishing truth in a moving world-order.

Further, such decisiveness makes short shrift of the follies of that sort of relativity doctrine which would say of any man or group of men that his inherited faith is "good enough for him," and presumably fits him better than any new one. No religion is good enough for any man but the true and universal religion; and if it is true and universal, it will fit every man under all circumstances. If there is any man or group of men whom Christianity does not fit, Christianity is a failure: it can be no final faith for anybody. Such fitness or unfitness can never be determined except by experiment. And a half-way experiment is no experiment. No one can learn whether wine suits him by mixing it with milk. The experiment must be clean.

So far, we have stated the case for the policy of radical displacement: it is a strong case. It has the further strength that it is independent of any appeal to visible results. If its four assumptions stand, the believer is bound to obedience whether there are any results or not. Of this attitude the Cambridge mission in Delhi and the Oxford mission in Calcutta are eminent examples: in terms of the number of converts they might at one time have been marked down as total failures; they have steadily refused to accept that measure of success. And so of the stone wall of Islam; for the conversions among Moslems, especially in the Near East and in northern Africa, are practically nil.*

Nevertheless, one cannot wholly avoid being aware of consequences, and of the argument which they press upon our working hypotheses. If there are no "results"; if there are bad results; if bad results mingle with good results, one is driven to reconsider his methods. And in respect to this way of Radical Displacement, there are consequences which have long raised doubts, not among the critics of missions alone, but among their friends. In what follows I shall rely in the main upon the experience of the mission, and the self-judgment of missionaries, who are their own most searching critics.

First, the total accomplishment of upward of a century of modern effort, after the all but complete failure of earlier missions to Asia: what is this result, in crude statistical terms? We know that the results of missions are not measured by statistics; we know (what is quite different) that many of the most important results never find their way into statistics; we know, too, that there are always latent results which *will* appear in statistics—such as the slow turning of

* A missionary to the Moslems writes in the *Moslem World* (July, 1937) to urge the virtue of patience, which, he says, means a "rugged determination not to be turned aside by opposition or seeming lack of result . . . Abraham had patience . . . why not we?" The analogy may not be coercive; but the principle is sound, on the premises noted.

large groups like an invisible ripening—but are at present to be reckoned as nothing. Allowing for all these things, the story of the figures is not to be rejected as meaningless; nor do the missions pretend indifference to them. Over long time, spirit takes to itself a commensurate body.

In India, roughly $1\frac{2}{3}$ per cent of the population are listed as Christian; in China three-quarters of 1 per cent; in Japan, just under half of 1 per cent. Of Protestant Christians (to whom alone the "century of modern effort" applies), there are estimated to be in India $2\frac{1}{2}$ million, or two-thirds of 1 per cent; in China six hundred thousand, or one-seventh of 1 per cent; in Japan, two hundred and ten thousand, or one-third of 1 per cent.

Of the volume of comment which these data invite, we must content ourselves with the barest. There are results. There is a Christian community in each of these lands. If we bear in mind the extraordinary effect upon Asiatic life made during the same period by other aspects of western culture, scientific, technical, legal, the advance made by the Christian community seems far from commensurate. Nor has the rate of advance maintained itself of recent years (except possibly in India): it is not following the law of geometrical increase which a vigorous and expanding life might be expected to show.

We turn to more significant matters.

What of the quality or power of the converts? It is natural that most of them should come from the masses, from workers rather than from the intellectuals; in India from the depressed groups. But as time passes should not the newer converts be a stronger group than the early ones? The reverse seems to be the case. It is one of the best known missionaries in India who made the following statement to us in 1931:

> It is a remarkable fact that the outstanding Christians in India are first generation: Sadhu Sundar Singh, Rama-bhai, etc. We had thought that the third and fourth generations would be much more outstanding (but what are the facts?) . . .
>
> The reason why these first generation people were wonderful was that they brought over their Hindu culture, and they were at home in their own categories. They had their roots back in their cultural past, therefore they were natural. The second generation was *taken out*, and became neither good Europeans nor good Indians. The second and third generation Christians are neither this nor that. In that period, the Indian Christian had lost his soul. A nationalist said to me: "Your Indian Christian is a man out of gear: he isn't in gear with your people, and he is out of gear with us."*

The quality of the convert is bound to be affected by the fact that the radical displacement must mean for him the abandonment of old loyalties. Consider the history of the treatment by Christian missions of the deep-seated custom of ancestor reverence in China and Korea.

> It is a well-known bit of history how the early Jesuit missionaries of the sixteenth and seventeenth centuries, led by Ricci, inclined to respect this custom and to admit it into Christian practice; and how after struggles between different groups of Catholics and apparent changes of mind

* An Indian who had been brought up in a Scotch mission remarked to President Edgar Park of Wheaton College, "I am not an Indian any more: I'm just a big black Scotchman!"

on the part of the Holy See, the controversy was ended in 1742 by the decree of Pope Benedict XIV, *"Ex Quo Singulari"*: No concessions were to be made to the customary practices of China. When the Protestant missionaries came, they followed as a rule the same prohibition, but with an added touch of decisiveness; the convert must *burn his ancestral tablets*, as a part of his explicit abjuring of the old faith and all its works, his "fierce 'No.' "

What happened in many cases is well put by a Korean Christian, Mr. Y. T. Pyun, in *My Attitude Toward Ancestor Worship*, an observance which, as he rightly explains, is in theory not worship at all, but rather "ancestor commemoration." I quote some of his quaint words:

The missionaries "kept their own society, clung to their own forms of worship. They did not dare think otherwise than that their own ways would exactly do the Koreans the same good. They never gave serious consideration upon the things which had been taking place for thousands of years among the people to whom they came as perfectors and teachers. . . . Ancestor worship was one of the things swept away by the avalanche of condemnation, and never duly reconsidered. It has been made a fundamental condition for a proselyte to forgo this abomination first." Then instances:

One Korean woman struggling with this requirement "felt uneasy even to the degree of sinfulness.

"One morning she took down all the ancestral tablets and threw them into the fire. While she was burning the objects which had been so long bound together with her reverence and gratitude toward her ancestors, she felt she was doing a great dishonour to their memory (even suffering an hallucination that she could hear their cries of pain and reproach). She became one of the *dragging Christians*." To her death she suffered a remorse which kept her from joy in her new faith.

Pyun comments on the psychological error of this

demand: "*Catch men alive*. If you hunt wild horses for hide you may use a gun; if for work, use a soft lassoo. . . . You cram your dear child with religious forms he does not comprehend (robbing him of those he has made his own) and afterwards become contrite at finding him devitalised in the faith!"

The cost of radical displacement to individuals in terms of personal suffering is not a decisive matter:* its moral cost is a more serious concern, when it tells in this way upon the fabric of the church. And there is another cost; namely the *loss of cultural fertility*, when the old roots of art and literature are cut. A valid conversion should result in a release of initiative and productivity, and a new freedom of imagination. In these qualities the new Churches of Asia have been singularly deficient. Under the policy we are discussing, they are like persons who have undergone a major surgical operation: they are saved to existence, but not to a normal vitality.† How can it be otherwise?

* These personal difficulties are accentuated in Moslem lands, where the converts are few and the Church largely of European membership. The position of the converts is clearly put by Harold B. Smith:

"Deprived of means of livelihood within their own community the converts turn to the Mission expecting employment. . . . They become helpers, Bible men and women, evangelists and pastors. They are expected to show qualities in keeping with these positions. When they prove unable to live up to these standards, sympathy all too soon gives way to criticism, understanding to misunderstanding, and the convert having voluntarily relinquished the comparative security of his former social surroundings, too frequently finds himself the object of mistrust and blame on the part of those in whom he may have expected to find real brothers. In more than one case of which I have known personally, highly sensitive youths have broken under the strain." (*Moslem World*, January 1939, pp. 24 f.)

† Hinduism has a rich heritage to draw upon in Art, Literature, Customs, etc. It can use these as media to convey the message of a reformed Hinduism to the masses.

"Christianity (in India) has no such heritage to rely upon: it is a stranger.

The question I raise is whether these consequence are not *necessary results of the method*. Radical displacement, with its purely negative attitude toward the old ways, must mean a degree of non-intercourse. It must bring about what is given the gentle name of "foreignness," the harder name of "deracination," the accurate name of "insulation." It must build an insulated church, holding an insulated doctrine,* and building an insulated community which is more like a foreign colony than an integral member of these newly self-conscious nations.

The economic implications of this policy are difficult, and have not infrequently led to its breakdown. If converts are to be separated from the old mode of life, including its economic activities, other modes of livelihood must be provided. This responsibility falls upon the mission, and gave rise in various lands to the once familiar institution of the "mission compound," partly for clear designation of property, partly for protection, partly for offering some attachment to the uprooted converts. But any such provision must have its limits. The converts were in effect dependents; the difference between the value of their marketable

Its equipment consists of Church History of the West, imported theology, western organization, and the inspiration of early missionaries and converts in the land. With these as its assets it is helpless to make itself one with the country."—A. N. Sudarisanam, 1939.

* The preaching of the Churches tends to insulate itself for this reason from local problems, and so to lose the interest of those who are immersed in them. Kagawa lamented (1932) that seventy per cent of the churches in Japan had no young men. His own converts join the churches, go in good hope, listen to the preaching, weary of it and drop away. Kagawa's comment is, "They want to help Japan."

products and the cost of their living had to be made up by the mission, and that meant ultimately by foreign subsidy at so much *per capita*. Hence the compound always reached the point at which no more converts *on that basis* could be accepted. And a change of basis carried with it a partial abandonment of the principle.

But even a partial success of this ideal of community self-sufficiency involves a sharp demarcation of the convert group from the rest of the society. In a nationally conscious state, such a group must become politically suspect. They have taken on something of the habits and mentality of their European mentors and guides. They are made aware of this, and find themselves at a disadvantage in offering any criticisms of public policy. If they yield to this disadvantage they cease to that extent to be citizens, and their new faith ceases to play its normal part in public debate.

There is a parallel difficulty in respect to all social co-operation, a point in which a Christian community should be fitted to render conspicuous aid. The idea of radical come-outness cannot align itself with the new social demands. It finds difficulty of principle in co-operating with Buddhist, Shintoist, Hindu authorities in a common attack on any social evil; and indeed when these authorities now recognise a social evil they prefer to deal with it themselves, rather than share credit with the foreign agency and the foreign ideas. In turn, social services maintained by the Radical Displacement missions thus tend to be such as they can conduct by themselves, and in conjunction with their own religious teaching. This tends to primitivise the Christian community; giving it a bent to economic and social simplicity; founding itself on agriculture and home arts. It is thus confirmed in its disposition to live apart, and now, in India, it is obliged by the new constitution to vote apart.

I repeat that these consequences are now everywhere resisted by the living missions; they are hastening to overcome the curse of foreignness with which they are stigmatised*; they are seeking to co-operate with leaders of the indigenous religions, and are thus recognising the moral authority of those leaders and the reality of their faiths. What I point out is that in so doing they are *defining another position*, inconsistent with that of Radical Displacement; and that what is admitted in practice must be admitted also in theory.

Meantime, the fruits of the original theory are present in the actual position of the Christian churches in Asia. I shall mention some examples of the insulation which they first built, and which public feeling now imposes on them.

ILLUSTRATIONS OF VARIOUS ASPECTS OF INSULATION

In Hangchow there are thirteen churches within a stone's throw of each other with a total of 1500 members. Dr. H. C. Wong, a Christian of the third generation,

* Speaking of the Christians of the younger Churches, Dr. Kraemer says: "The more thoughtful amongst them are grievously troubled by the foreignness of Christianity, and feel much in it to be unnecessarily foreign and antagonistic to the atmosphere of their own cultural background. Their souls are aspiring after an indigenous expression of Christianity that will deliver their religion from the blighting curse of foreignness." (Op. cit., p. 318).

American in education, dress, accent, "discovered after 25 years that he was a Chinese," and was disturbed by the saying of a Chinese pastor, "More a Christian, less a Chinese." He conceived the idea of a Christian Church expressing the Chinese spirit in architecture, music, etc., for "western music does not stir the Chinese soul." In November 1931 he went to the authorities asking for registration and permission to build. "Show us your American charter." Answer: "This is a Chinese enterprise." Application refused: to the authorities a Christian church was by its nature a foreign enterprise. Dr. Wong finally won his charter.

The Wesleyan church at Medak, one of the most queenly buildings in India in position and architecture, is seen as one approaches the rim of the magnificent valley, standing out like an English cathedral. It is approached through a glorious formal garden, diligently kept by native hands. This is one of the finest Indian churches; yet typical in this, that western purses and western builders must keep it up. It could not conceivably become an Indian institution.

The great cotton mills in Ahmedabad, Indian owned and managed, were left by their founder to a son and a daughter whose policies toward employes were far apart; he was for a twelve-rupee wage, she for eighteen. They brought the question to Gandhi, then in his Sabarmati ashram: his reply was "Peace depends on justice." He proposed a system of arbitration prompt and efficient, under a Hindu judge. A club house was established for the workers. Each evening disputes arising during the day were there reviewed and disposed of. During twenty years there had been (1931) but two minor strikes. An element of Hindu social sense and religion enters into the spirit of the place. This remark was made by one of the owners: "During these twenty years, no missionary has visited the place. . . . A mission college opened a course on industrial relations. I wrote with diffidence to the Principal, saying that if any members of their staff desired to visit, they would be welcome. . . . Reply: 'Our own resources are sufficient.' "

A medical missionary in Ceylon, after a life of service, wrote me as follows:

We have been there a hundred years, and we seem as far as ever from being able to move out and leave the work to the Ceylonese. What is the matter? If after a hundred years we cannot bequeathe it to them, when in God's name can we? It is as though we had remained outside the springs of their minds, content with administering surface plasters. Our work and our ideas simply haven't *taken*. Either we are trying to do the impossible—make silk purses out of sows' ears—in which case the whole basis of our work is mistaken; or there is something radically wrong in our way of teaching. We are chronic outsiders.

In sum, no one can say of the Church in Asia, that it has as a whole become indigenous, in the sense that its western sponsors feel it safe to leave it to its own growth. There are many spots where it has taken root. There is a real church in Korea; there is (or was) an activity of evangelism in Shantung carried on by Chinese Christians; there is genuine initiative in portions of central India; there are points of life in Japan. But it is not clear how many even of these living centres would survive the withdrawal of foreign support; whereas it is clear that the great body of the younger churches would not.

And as the prestige of the western nations which

has hitherto supported these colonies in their uncomfortable status tends to decline, with the rise of self-conscious, self-differentiating Asiatic power, the position of these Christian colonies, drawn largely from the lower classes, tends to resemble that of the ancient Jewish diaspora. By a strange reversal of fates, the native Christian might conceivably become the international Jew of Asia.

If the method of Radical Displacement were consistently followed, some such result would be probable. It is not consistently followed. But the method itself which produces these results is seldom expressly criticised; there is nowhere an adequate diagnosis of the source of the malady. In my judgment, its pedagogy is defective, and the psychology underlying it; and these defects trace to the untenable character of the presuppositions themselves.

I shall refer first to the psychological symptoms, and then consider the root of the difficulty.

Radical Displacement is animated by the belief that the faith to be conveyed is complete in itself. It requires no contributions from the surrounding world of ideas; the duty of the preacher is to transmit it intact and with fidelity. The formulae of the faith are the vessels in which it may be most safely conveyed. There are perils in attempts to make it relevant not alone to the issues of the outer world, but even to the specific questions of the convert.

This involves defiance of an inescapable principle of teaching: *nothing can be conveyed to any mind unless it answers that mind's own questions.* The insulated doctrine is a talent wrapped in a napkin and buried in the earth; and the anxious care for faithful transmission which expects to report: "Lo, here thou hast that is thine," must be pronounced inadequate to the living situation. The working principle is, Nothing can be conveyed unless it undergoes the peril of growth.

A striking instance of this is seen in an episode in connection with a Chinese translation of the Methodist Book of Discipline and Ritual. The story may best be told by a Methodist missionary resident in China:

Prior to the last revision the Apostle's Creed appeared in the Chinese version as an exact translation of the English. Following our General Conference in America, the East Asia Conference, meeting in 1925, authorised a new translation of the Discipline and Ritual to be made, conforming to changes made by the General Conference of 1924. Needless to say no changes had been made in the Apostle's Creed by the General Conference. However, the Chinese committee appointed to carry out the revised translation into Chinese took it upon themselves to man-handle the Creed, breaking it up into eight questions to be answered by the applicant for baptism: this Committee included several returned students, who apparently felt that their American degrees entitled them to revise the historic creeds of the Church. Their new translation slipped through without being checked, and thus it appears in all our (Chinese) Books of Discipline and Ritual published since 1926. Our preachers have paid little attention to the change, as the average Chinese pastor doesn't worry much about theological problems. The eight questions put in place of the Creed are as follows:

Do you believe in God, the Heavenly Father?
Do you believe that Jesus Christ is the only-begotten holy Son of God?

Do you believe that the Holy Spirit is man's guide, that which makes him righteous?

Do you believe in salvation from sin, and in liberation from sin's power of death?

Do you believe in the development of Christ's Kingdom of Peace and Harmony, by means of the Holy Church?

Do you believe that His love and righteousness in the end will be victorious?

Do you believe in eternal life after death?

Do you wish, with the help of the Lord, to carry out His holy will and commandments, with all your strength and throughout your life?

This last question is additional to the substance of the Creed, whose propositions are thus drafted off into seven questions, to be answered by the word of assent. The omissions are notable—all the career of Jesus from "conceived of the Holy Ghost, born of the Virgin Mary" to the Ascension and the Second Coming "to judge the quick and the dead"—also the "Communion of Saints, the Resurrection of the Body." There are also notable additions, in the form of explanatory clauses.

Perhaps equally instructive is the long period during which this high-handed mutilation of the ancient symbol remained unnoticed by the western sponsors, and during which the Chinese Church appeared to be none the worse for the scandal! It was at least a brave attempt to break through the capsule of an insulated doctrine.

And as for the underlying psychology. It is true that man has an incredible capacity to change, and not infrequently an appetite for changing: the artificial man is the rule, rather than the exception, in the sense of the man who has constructed his own moral physiognomy; cultural conversion is always possible. But if, in these conversions, there is a *turning away from an* *ancient good* as well as from an ancient evil, there will remain in the individual, and still more in the group, a residual strain. The subconscious self cannot accept the radical otherness which the conscious self has adopted. There will be a harking-back, *a cultural homesickness*, asserting itself in movements of reversion. There is a need of emotional rootedness which the intellect never does full justice to.* There is need for a living base in a consciousness which is not self-consciously effortful, even while the dramatised part is being perfectly played. The only conversion not subject to regression is conversion to a mode of being which can interpret *all* the valuable elements of the old mode.

ILLUSTRATION

K——— K——— was a capable Japanese student of metaphysics when I first knew him. He had come to us from a theological seminary near by.

I asked him why he had wanted additional metaphysics; was not theology metaphysics? His answer was, the theology he had been taught was too clear! Everything was provided for; it was all definite. He missed the sense of infinity, of mystery, to which he had been accustomed as a boy. He told me his story.

He came of a Tendai Buddhist family of northern Japan, where his uncle was chief priest in a temple high up in the mountain in a grove of great trees. He himself had

* In this respect, some of the earlier missions were both wiser and kinder than the missions of Displacement. It was Pope Gregory who instructed Augustine on his mission to England: "Destroy the idols, but keep the temples, so that when the people come to their accustomed places it may be with a feeling of being at home." (Professor Roderick Scott.)

been destined to succeed to the high priesthood. He could hear in his home, early in the morning, the sound of the temple gongs; and he knew that the priests were seated before the images of the Buddha, and were reciting the sutras. After this, they would retire each one to his own cell, to spend the morning in meditation and study. These monk-priests used their time well; they had read their European philosophy as well as their Buddhist scriptures; they knew their Kant, Schleiermacher, Schopenhauer, Hegel. He recalled with some regret that the missionaries did not know these thinkers, and could not converse on equal terms with the monks. Why?

In part, because they were too busy. They had pastoral duties which the monks did not have. The monks would not go into the houses of the people; they would see those who came to them. Then the missionaries had much time to spend in making reports. They gave the impression of persons always hurried, always harassed by many duties, devoid of repose, devoid of inner peace, devoid of opportunity to cultivate the sense of depth, solemnity, mystery in the vast world, which more and more became to him an essential of religion.

He had been converted by a missionary to whom he looked up on account of his noble personal character; and for whom he now began to feel a certain sentiment of pity and lack.

He was wondering whether Christianity was, after all, relatively thin, schematic, doctrinal, over-rationalized. He was suffering from religious and cultural homesickness, and not without reason.

I asked him whether he had not read the Christian mystics. He seemed not to know them. So I put into his hand a copy of *Theologia Germanica* and asked him to read it on the steamer. Not everything in Christianity was "too clear."

No church has any interest in making masses of imitative, hollow Christians, wearers of masks which give them the expression of less than their full personalities. The mission desires to give life to the whole soul of the East, not to part of it. It has to save the social and political conscience; it has to save its history; and not alone its individual present. If Christianity cannot do this, it cannot come forward as their necessary religion. If Christianity does accept this task, it owes to itself a redefinition of what it means by conversion, and what it means by the obligatory elements in its own faith.

We turn therefore to consider the religious groundwork of this method of Radical Displacement.

REVIEW OF PRESUPPOSITIONS

1. *Special Revelation.*—The method of Radical Displacement is based first of all on the belief that however God may have disclosed himself to man in the general appointments of nature and history, and perhaps here and there dimly to the great sages, he has so specifically and definitely spoken through the Bible and through Jesus Christ that this channel of truth must displace or take precedence of all others. Such revelation is explicitly different from all deliverances of human insight or reason, such as reflection reaches. It conveys, in particular, the plan of salvation which is not in any sense a product of thought, not

even of God's thought; it is a deed of God's will, His good will to men. This revelation comes as an announcement, a word of good news, without reference to the human context or prior questioning, a discontinuity, an irruption into history of something which history itself could not have generated.

What is the evidence for this doctrine?

Either the content of revelation commends itself to ·the human receiver through its intrinsic quality, or it does not. If it does so commend itself, it comes within human apprehension, and the gulf it was sought to establish between it and the human reach begins to be bridged. If the gulf is to be maintained, we are driven to the other alternative—that the content of revelation does not commend itself to reason; it not only exceeds, but in a sense rebukes the best devices of human thought. This is the position toward which the advocates of this doctrine tend by necessity.

> So Karl Barth. Revelation is not an idea which we can think out, it is an event which has happened, "with the complete once-for-all singularity (Einmaligkeit) and with the whole gravity of a factual event." It is "an event of the free and sovereign activity of God toward man." It is not a union or fusion of God and man; it is not a meeting in which "man can appear and co-operate as God's partner"; "it is not founded on the ambiguous truth of our human nature, reason, or love." It is a gift of God Himself: "it is a truth which cannot be measured by the rule of any other truth beside it, however profound and valid that truth may appear to be." Revelation is an event because it is an act. "That it is an event we are told by the biblical witnesses."*

> * *God in Action*, pp. 4, 7, 13, 19.

Thus also Dr. Kraemer:

> The crucial fact on which alone a missionary movement can rest is "that God has revealed *the* Way in Jesus Christ and wills this to be known through all the world." The conviction that this is the case is not to be defended by argument; it is a matter of faith. "Ultimate convictions never rest on a universally lucid and valid argument. To adhere to a certain view of life has always meant a choice and a decision."*

If we adhere strictly to the language of these utterances—that there is no communicable evidence for revelation, that it is an affair of decision based on subjective assent—then this, the most important of all truths, is left to an essentially occult apprehension, and the world of religions becomes a confusion of different deciders who have no means of rational conversation. Yet Christians of this persuasion should, on their own showing, be busy in sending missions not alone to the non-Christians but also to Christians of every other view than their own.

> This is the wholly logical position of the Catholic tradition. During a conversation in Darjeeling with a leading Jesuit about the position of Christianity in India, I asked this question: "When we Protestants count the Christians of India, we include the Catholics with the Protestants; when you count the Christians of India, do you include the Protestants with the Catholics?" The answer, delivered with all urbanity and all definiteness, was "No; why should we?"

I submit that we must indeed take the question of truth seriously, far more seriously than any self-stulti-

* *The Christian Message*, p. 107.

fying circle whose ultimate apology is, "I believe because I decide to believe." We must go behind what
the advocates of special revelation say, to what one
must judge they mean. They cannot mean that the
question, What is the will of God? has to be answered
as a purely historical question of fact into which we
have no insight—as if God had one day devised a
plan for the redemption of fallen man, and then one
day announced it in a miraculous manner—this
announcement having been conveyed to our minds
through the centuries by wholly reliable transmitters
whose message we have but to receive in obedience as
an incomprehensible gift. They cannot mean this.

They are engaged, I believe, in making an important
distinction between a type of truth which is thought
out, and a type of truth which lies beyond excogitation,
which has to be discovered, and by each man for
himself. Revelation belongs to the latter type; and this
may offer a clue to a tenable understanding of that
term.

In religious knowledge, as in other knowledge, there
is a part which comes, as we say, from experience.
Thus, the knowledge of God is not first a matter of
pure reason; God is a name which we give to the felt
difference between a living and a dead world: we know
by direct experience that the cosmos is the sort of
entity toward which a sense of obligation is appropriate.
God is, in this sense, "revealed"; and revelation in the
broadest sense is the empirical element in religious
knowledge. It does not exclude thought, but it lies
beyond what thought alone could offer, just as all

knowledge of what actually exists lies beyond the
scope of thought. It is something which "I find to
be so."

In a special sense, revelation is concerned with our
knowledge of the will of God. How do we know the
will of God? In the Greek conception, if God could be
said to have a will at all, it could only be a timeless
preference for the Good, the Beautiful, and the True.
And we know the will of God as we know these Ideas.
Now we need not doubt that God has eternal preferences; nor that these terms roughly indicate some of
them; nor that—since we human beings dimly understand these terms—the will of God is to that extent
revealed to us. But eternal preferences do not constitute
a *will*: they are principles of will rather than will
itself. For will has reference to time, to action, to
history. If God has will, he is concerned with time and
acts in time.

This is one of the important elements in the theory
of special revelation: it insists that God acts, and reveals
Himself in events. If the temporal world is God's deed,
in any sense, then in that sense all that happens comes
within the scope of his temporal concern. And in a
special sense, to each individual self, *his* world of
experience is a direct address of God to him. The cosmic
demand which comes to him that he consider his
individual life as a commission, in which the spread
of righteousness is to take place through his unique
action—this is an historic and particular aspect of
God's will. And there will be events in each life in
which not merely the existence of God but the quality
of God's being, will become peculiarly manifest.

Here again, God reveals Himself in the time-order. Thus for each individual person, his revelation is *his* Burning Bush; and his response to it is his response to objective, historical fact.

But such response is *never response to the arbitrary or unintelligible:* just the reverse. It is a response to a surcharge of meaning. It is a response to the presence of God: for revelation means that God becomes perceptible through the medium of experience in time. It is another aspect of "Incarnation"—God embodied in Fact; and incarnation is luminous, not opaque.

The true contrast is not between the intelligible (for reason) and the impenetrable (for faith); but between the purely general and ideal (for abstract reason) and the historical event surcharged with meaning for (receptive faith). To make the will of God a mystery of transcendental history to be submitted to in blind obedience, that is to make a merit of pure submission. It is to revel in the abasement of the human. It is to put Jesus in the wrong: for Jesus said not that we must unman ourselves to enter the Kingdom, but that we must become as little children— who are still human! It is to take a step backward out of Christianity toward a re-enslavement of the human soul.

The religions in which reason has a welcome place are in this respect higher than those in which only divine dicta are given out. We may go farther, for it is the nature of all religion to regard the human being as co-operating with the cosmic demand in his own concern for righteousness, and so far to participate in its meaning: we may say, then, that where the human participation is in principle excluded, and man's apprehension rebuffed, there is indeed abasement, but there is no religion at all.

The idea of a divine plan, considered as a dated product of God's wisdom and goodness wholly unimaginable to man, is, I fear, an ingenious invention of Saint Paul.* To take it up again to-day is to place a halter around the neck of Christianity for those to tug at who are disposed to work upon the more craven fears of the human heart. It is time for a robust and honest Christianity to have done with all this rattling of ancient moral chains.

2. *The Stake.*—For our forefathers there was a clear-cut issue: to them, salvation had a quite literal meaning, wholly other-worldly. It was the alternative to damnation, in a quite literal and perhaps imminent world-end and judgment. Damnation meant quite literal eternal punishment, eternal suffering, quite literal Hell. The "lostness" of the world which was without the one talisman of salvation consisted quite literally in its liability to this fate. The language of the Bible, even of Jesus, on whose lips frequent references to "wailing and gnashing of teeth" are reported, justified these images of the alternative. If we are to

---

* Saint Paul, as Professor Roderick Scott of Fukien College reminds me, has another side; and I have no wish to forget that the genius of this great preacher rose at times far above the level of the juristic analogies which he imported into theology. It was he who declared that God had not left himself without a witness, and who spoke of the universal revelation of God in nature. But in his systematic moments, this same Paul considered that such indulgence toward human kind was only for "the days of our ignorance" (Acts xvii); and that the era of grace was to be an era of a new legality.

accept "biblical realism" as a principle, there is no doubt where we must stand.

If we reject these images, as we all do,* we confess that we are taking our biblical realism with a grain of salt. In no respect has the theological atmosphere more unanimously and radically altered in the last fifty years. It has, I think, altered too much. It is too easily considered that, since Hell and the Devil have been outgrown, the realities of sin and its intrinsic punishment have been outgrown also; and that the moral gravamen of human decision has vastly lightened. There is a moral equivalent of Hell; and the issues of life and death still hang on our moral decisions. But the question we have to face is whether the line between life and death is drawn, in God's decision, between those who do know and follow the specific revelation in Christ and those who do not know it and follow it.

All the impressiveness and exhortation, all the solemnities of "Only Way" preaching, imply that the line is so drawn; and in Dr. Kraemer's view, this is "the only possible basis" for a missionary movement.

Yet I do not find in Dr. Kraemer's book any clear statement of what he conceives will happen to those who do not follow his prescribed path. I do not find any discussion of what the ultimate and grave alter-

---

* I had supposed prior to my visit to the Far East that the preaching of Hell had vanished from the modern mission field. It has not in all quarters. In a mission in Burma, a vigorous young missionary was warned by a friend not to dwell so much on Hell, because the Buddhists have eight hells, whereas the Christians have only one. His response was to change his preaching to this effect: "You have eight hells; we have but one; but we have a God who sees that you get there."

native is: although, as he must see, the significance of everything he says depends on this. Without clarity here, there is no literalness, and no realism.

This same fatal weakness appears to pervade the words of all those who now represent the method of Radical Displacement. It is as though they did not quite believe in the danger which they imply without defining. Their words have a hollow sound. They evade the issue, and run off into figures of speech.

> Examples: The directing head of a mission in Benares writes as follows of a Moslem tailor who was in the habit of rising at four, using two hours in prayer and reading the Koran before going to his day's work at the mission, which he did with fidelity and skill:
>
> "Truly the zeal and diligence of these men would put us Christians to shame. Please pray for this man, because no amount of asceticism and reading of any book save The Book will avail at the Judgment Seat of God." Avail for what?
>
> A similar veiled threat of punishment and exclusion is frequently conveyed by the simple word "necessary," without specifying for what the condition is necessary Thus Bishop Badley of Bombay (Methodist Mission), in drawing up a list of "essentials" mentions:
>
> "The necessity of experiencing Pentecost with the fulness of the Holy Spirit."
>
> This necessity appears to be very much a specialty of the good Bishop himself; but, necessary for what?

This hesitation, vagueness, and evasion mean, I believe, a creditable unwillingness to believe in a God whose justice is on a much lower level than one's own. But they also mean that a necessary prop of Radical

Displacement, the doctrine of the Only Way, is felt to be indefensible.

3. *The "Only Way."*—Without the two foregoing supports, the idea of the "Only Way" as it is taken by the advocates of Radical Displacement falls. There is no Only Way to God. There is no Only Way to salvation and peace.

> This result has been already implied in our original postulate regarding savedness and lostness; these conditions are not confined within the limits of any one religion. The verifiable aspect of savedness is discernible outside Christianity. The issue is not a new one. It dates to the second century of our era, to the debate between Marcion and the Apologists. Marcion, wealthy ship owner of Sinope on the Black Sea, was converted to Christianity—the only religion he had been interested in. He was completely won over. There was for him no other way. Stoics and Platonists were pretentious intellectuals, lost in vain pride of wit. The God of the Old Testament was a violent and evil power.
>
> The Apologists had cared for religion all their lives. They wanted to keep the Old Testament and to recognise the Sages and the Stoics. To them Christianity was not the newest religion, but the most ancient and most fundamental. The Church, by the end of the second century had to decide between these views, the Only Way view of Marcion, and that of the Apologists.
>
> It decided for the Apologists. Marcion, the Only Way exponent, was condemned as a heretic.*

The Barthian attempt to revive such exclusiveness is, with all its reinvigorating power, an evident failure at this point. The religions of Asia are not "wolves."

* W. D. Sperry.

Without attempting at this moment any appraisal of merit or defect, it must be said of them that they are religions, and as such, they are ways to God: they have with all their *laissez faire*, somnolence, passivity to popular superstition, done one great thing: they have kept the light of a true spirituality more or less vividly alive in Asia for tens of centuries.

There is indeed a sense in which we may speak of an Only Way: no way which is counter to Truth can be a valid way; no way which is inimical to Life can be valid—and there will always be more ways of going wrong than of going right—they are collectively the Broad Path. The way of Truth seems at times to pull counter to the way of Life; and we have rumour of "life-giving falsehoods," myths and fictions which one is to hold "as if true" for their pragmatic value. The arduous way which holds the Truth and the Life together is *the* Way, and there can be no other, in the sense of inconsistent, way.

But in the guise we have been considering, as an only way to God, this doctrine must be abandoned definitely and for all.

It was once a form of religious intensification, an emotional and dogmatic postulate pragmatically valuable, so long as it could be realistically believed. It has now become a perverse and injurious instrument for guiding the contact of religions, inflicting pain beyond the meaning of the occasion, intolerable in its intolerance. It is increasingly ineffective in winning souls who have learned that religion cannot be based on fear; but it is chiefly obnoxious to the ultimate sense of truth in the hearts of those who try to believe it.

Our conclusion in regard to the Method of Radical Displacement may be summarised:

1. The theological presuppositions of the method are no longer tenable; and the method itself, deprived of this support, becomes discredited. The complete discontinuity between old and new at which it aims is not in fact achievable. In so far as it is achieved, it works an individual loss of bearing, and tends to an insulation of doctrine, of church and of community, which compel the search for other alternatives.

If it were true, as is sometimes claimed, that without the doctrine of the Only Way missions lose their sufficient motive, I should accept that result: we cannot take it as a fixed premiss that missions must go on.* But I do not believe the argument. The evidence against it is that it is hard to find at present a pure example of this method anywhere in Asia. (The China Inland Mission approximates it); it is everywhere modified and thereby abandoned in principle—for a partial Only Way is no Only Way at all! But the abandonment in practice is not yet generally admitted in theory; this step must come.

The changed attitude implies that conversions under

* This premiss is made the basis of many a recent appeal for the Only Way theology; the general plan of the argument is this, that since missions must go on, and since the Only Way theology is the only theology that will sustain their motive, the Only Way theology must be adopted. This strange putting-the-cart-before-the-horse is understandable in persons deeply committed to the enterprise itself by habit or official relationship, so that the necessity of continuing missions has become for them a practical axiom. For us, the practical premiss is the broader one, that a world-faith must be achieved; and whether the mission, in some one of its various forms, is now the fit means to that end is the question in hand. Preaching is ancient and inseparable from religion itself; the modern Protestant mission is a very recent device.

the fear of eternal punishment for adhering to other
systems have become illegitimate conversions; and
that the elimination of other systems can no longer
be a part of the direct aim of the mission. The local
religions are exercising functions which Christianity
cannot yet undertake, and which it cannot relegate to
zero. The possibilities of relationship between Christianity and the other religions are far richer than the
simple one of hostile exclusiveness, with all its exhilar-
ation and its appeal to the love of clear-cut-ness. We
have yet to explore some other of these possibilities.

2. The way must be always open for persons who
wish as individuals to make the clean separation
between old and new modes of faith. There are always
athletic souls who can achieve the revolution and be
the stronger for it. And there are moments of ethical
upswing when whole groups appear ready for a new
definition of their world-outlook. This is especially
true of groups who have been depressed or long stagnant in speculative life, and who are capable as a group
of perceiving a better position, under the leadership of
their own authorities. There should be no bar to this
kind of change.

It is meaningless to talk of the relations between
Christianity and other religions in Asia unless there
is in Asia a Christian Church. And a Church cannot
exist unless it has its possibilities of accessions of
membership. The freedom of those discussions which
are incident to the attempt to convert mature persons
and groups from one faith to another is a part of the
health and liveliness of religion in any community;
so long as no unfair pressures or inducements are

used, and so long as the liberty to persuade is mutual the right to propagate one's faith should be provided for in every national constitution, and is a proper subject for international convention.

3. As a part of this freedom, the several churches must be free to maintain each one its own conception of the faith, including those who continue mistakenly to believe that they have the Only Way.

Men are, as a rule, better than their theologies. Under the guise of a ruthless Calvinism many an heroic individual has gone about doing good, with a union of dogmatic resolution, human competence, and inner benignity that have made his name a legend and a beacon. Fanaticism is an element of character and not alone of creed or organisation; and the world is not yet ready to dispense with the sometimes glorious fanaticisms of the narrower faiths. I am prepared to fight for the right of the bigots to do the missionary work they feel impelled to do. But I hope for their conversion; I am still more inclined to fight for the rights of the human soul to its full freedom and stature, and the just relation of the great religious communities. We turn to consider a second way to a world faith; that of Synthesis.

2

THE WAY OF SYNTHESIS

WHEN two religions are present in the same region,
each tends to adopt from the other whatever seems
peculiarly expressive in its language or significant
in its ways, whether deliberately or by a less conscious
kind of appropriation. There is mutual teaching and
learning; and since this process involves incorporating
with one's own religion certain elements of other
religions, we may call it Synthesis.*

This way is an aspect of Liberalism. It is liberal in
the sense of being unwilling to condemn as evil what
is good in other faiths. It considers both sides of the
admonition of Isaiah: "Woe unto them that call
evil good, and good evil!"† It is fairly easy to observe
the first half of this injunction by a purist policy which
avoids all touch of otherness; that is an incident of
the Radical Displacement method. But this method

* Other names have been used for this way, though they have become
ambiguous by applying also to ways superficially resembling "Synthesis."
"Eclecticism" should be reserved for the process of starting a new religion
composed of a medley of ingredients from several others. This word is in
deserved bad odour; but since it is less appealed to, it excites less horror
than the word "syncretism," which now carries the flavour of theological
promiscuity. To be suspected of "syncretism" is to be accused of a peculiarly poisonous variety of heresy. In itself it is an entirely respectable name
for a process repeatedly exemplified in the early history of Christianity.
But since it is now a term of reproach in a field in which there are various
possible abuses awaiting proper labels, we may regretfully leave it to its
destiny.

† Isaiah v. 20.

shuns or condemns as evil much that is good, and so falls foul of the second half of the warning. This the Liberal is solicitous for: he fears the wholesale exclusions which cast the shadow of evil on something of value. In this respect, the liberal temper is a direct offshoot of Christianity; it is an extension of the love for one's neighbour, since a concern for the individual implies a regard for his attachments and his reverence. It is an aspect of "loyalty to loyalty"; it fears the wounds made by unnecessary abandonment of old ties as it fears the lesions of divorce. It is not an accident that the comparative study of religions has grown and flourished chiefly in Christian lands.

This method has obvious dangers. There is the danger of compromise through over-accommodation. Led by a desire, among other things, to make oneself intelligible to others of different traditions by speaking their language, and coming as far as possible into their world of thought, one is likely to adopt terms and concepts surcharged with connotations inconsistent with one's meaning.

Translators of the Bible are commonly torn by this dilemma. If we use for "God" the Chinese term Tien or Shang Ti, we shall use a term understood, but also a term which has its own history and suggestions. If we insist on the term "God," we impose from the first a puzzle or a blank where one wants to rely on a spontaneous and natural understanding. And, after all, "God" is English, not Hebrew nor Greek! Chiang Kai Shek is said to have called for a new Chinese translation of the Bible purified of Confucian terminology. Dr. Richter surmises that the slowness with which Christianity has been absorbed by the German people may be due to imperfect translations: for the Greek *metanoein* they took the word *Busse*, and thus misled their minds for centuries on the nature of the Atonement. He says that this "danger of using terms the connotation of which is adulterating the Christian mind even after generations is particularly lurking in languages which through millenniums have been impregnated by connotations in the wrong direction."

There is the danger of purely romantic appreciation, which on the basis of slight impressions, without the curing influence of long acquaintance and experience impulsively pronounces as good what may have a root in evil.

There is the danger of moral and mental idleness, the soft indisposition to face issues, first scrupulously defining them. To announce "We agree," when we also differ, is not conspicuously truer nor more politic than to put forward "We differ" when we also agree. In either case the labour of differing has to be accomplished.

All toleration has its malaise, that in being kind to what is not one's own, one is subtly disloyal to one's own. To consider hospitably what an opponent believes is to loosen attachment to what one has already professed to believe; it is to depress into the region of controversy and hypothesis what was once in the region of certainty and conviction. All the gods are jealous; and some are legitimately jealous, namely those that deserve an unqualified, unclouded, unwavering assent. He who surrenders the absoluteness and finality of his primary loyalty is like the broadminded traveller who has surrendered his patriotism and has no country, or like the broadminded thinker whose brain is a sieve into which everything may run though nothing can be retained and owned. This is the intrinsic curse of the "liberal" attitude, whether in theology or elsewhere; it is the price sometimes paid for swiftness of sympathy with the alien "point of view," and when it means no decision, no selfhood, no limit to tentative concession, the price is too great. Need it be too great?

There are so many examples in the world of a breadth acquired by relaxation that the antipathy to "syncretism" is intelligible. The various movements to unite religions in "one vast harmony"; the Parliament of Religions attitude, ready to represent in its assemblage anything that presents itself as a religion, fair and foul alike; the several newer religions undertaking to be universal by liberal selection, all such are infertile aggregates. The sense of artefact hangs over them all.*

* Theosophy, Bahaism, "Unity," come, to some extent, under this category though each has a distinctive nucleus of doctrine.

As an example of eclecticism, such as one finds in various new cults in China and elsewhere, let me describe the Tao Yuan Society as one finds it (or found it) in Tsinanfu. This society honours five religious founders: Confucius, Lao Tze, Buddha, Jesus, Mohammed. Behind these founders there is a unitary principle which is called the Laotzu (not Laotze): Laotzu means "old ancestor." It differs from the idea of Tao in including an element of personality. It represents an object of devotion common to all religions. It is the origin of the universe. It differs from the idea of the Father God in the respect that man is related to this origin only indirectly.

The Society is organized both for worship and for philanthropy. It has its own rituals and its own tablets. It conducts a number of philanthropic enterprises in Tsinan. We were admitted to look at its place of worship, a place without images, but with an altar containing a central niche in which, instead of the usual tablet, there appeared to be a photographic plate obscurely blotched. Underneath this niche there was a row of five niches, each with a

They are well enough symbolised by the mantleshelf of an Indian reconciler of faiths on which were brought together for adoration figures of Siva and Buddha, a crucifix, a portrait scroll of Confucius and a bust of W. E. Gladstone! There is no vital breath in such agglomerates because there is no self. One flies from them for relief to the fiercer sectarianism which at least has character enough to know what it excludes. A religion must *be* something before it can take on anything as part of itself.

All these dangers are there: but they simply sharpen the question, *What is the legitimate process of Synthesis?* For there is a normal process, which has to be distinguished from its counterfeits.

And this question is equivalent to the question, Is

murky plate within it. We were interested to learn that the upper plate was a photographic impression of Laotzu, the old ancestor, made by himself through spiritual means, and that the five lower glasses contained portraits of the five religious founders, produced in the same esoteric way.

In an adjoining room there was a group of people engaged in a solemn enterprise, whose nature we shortly discovered. We were led around by another door and found a railing behind which two Chinese were holding opposite ends of a rod of about five feet in length, from whose lower edge projected a long wooden prong touching a square pan of sand; and as the arms of these two devotees were moved, the lower finger traced in the sand lines which turned out to be Chinese characters.

A third member stood by, announced the character when completed, and swept it out by a swift movement of a piece of board, leaving the sand clear for another tracing. A fourth member was a recorder, who took down the letters as they appeared and construed the resulting sentences. This was the most lively and consecutive consultation of the spirits that I have yet witnessed. There was no pause, and the two pole swingers were as active as if they had been sawing wood at the opposite ends of a cross-cut saw. The products of this spiritualist device were recorded—five substantial volumes of ethical instruction, the nucleus of a new, modern and best of all, joint revelation from the common spirit of all the sacred founders.

there growth in religion? For legitimate synthesis is growth, and growth through recognizing one's proper food. Is it, after all, a matter of choice whether one recognises an idea, held by someone else, as a true idea, and as one which belongs to oneself by virtue of fitting-in-with and developing what one has hitherto thought? Perhaps we would better ask, *can such growth be prevented* except by a resolute living in blinders? Has not truth its imperative "both-and" as well as its imperative "either-or"?

In the point of experience we find precisely this to be the crux of the matter. The price of non-growth is an almost unachievable ignorance of the other systems. Fear of contamination by alien ideas, together with a conviction that one's own faith has everything desirable, has brought some few (chiefly Protestant) missionaries close to this ideal. In the notion of the complete and finished deposit of faith there is nothing to drive the complacent Messenger into the arduous path of investigating the ways of the "wolves." But the distinguished work done by many of the early Protestant missionaries and by numerous later ones in the field of oriental scholarship shows that such complacency, where it exists, is a matter of accident rather than of principle.

As a principle, it could set up a strong defence; but the defence would put an end to the mission. It would read as follows: All religious and social systems are organic; each idea and custom carries the colour of the whole system of which it is a part. Hence ideas and practices which seem nominally alike are not alike; the words for God, sin, etc., do not mean the same in any two systems. There are no equivalents. This is literally true. But the consequences are disastrous. There can be no translations; there should be none. The Bible ought never to have been put into Latin, nor into any other language than its own! The resistance which Islam has maintained to the translations of the Koran has had this just foundation. Until the recent extraordinary activity in translating on the part of the Ahmadiyya variant of Islam, commonly regarded as heretical, it was customary to disguise a translation of the Koran as an "explanation" in other terms, and such translations were few. More than this, on the same ground, there should be *no conversation* with those of alien faith, or in other than the original languages! The scruple is unanswerable except by its own impossible implications: it is self-defeating. It fails by the simple necessities of intercourse among living things, including such intercourse as aims to convert.

What, then, are the criteria of a legitimate synthesis? They are: Individuality, organic unity, consistency.

Individuality: The religion which grows by accretion must have a recognisable being or character of its own to begin with, and must retain that individuality through the process of growth. The borrowed elements must not efface or neutralise that character.

Organic unity: What is added must not remain extraneous, like an ornament or a piece of baggage, but must become a part of the organism of the living religion.

Consistency: What is thus entertained must be

consistent with what is there. The chief complaint against the wide hospitalities of Hinduism has been that its adopted ingredients may be at war with one another, morally and logically.

But all of these are comprised in one: the *truth of what is adopted*. For if a religion has aimed at truth, and if truth is of its own nature self-consistent and organic, then any new region of truth will be consistent and organic with the truth already there. And if inconsistency appears, it may be the older version that needs to be changed. If it can be changed within the limits of the same selfhood, the new may safely be incorporated with the old.

The inadmissible syntheses are those which attempt to unite truth and error, right and wrong, God and mammon; these are the choices which call for the stern Either-Or of decision.

But it is not open to any little man to announce that *his* "Either-Or" must be taken as the decisive thing. We have been called upon, within living memory, to "choose this day" between Genesis and Evolution, between the Bible and Modern Science, much to the confusion of our judgment, and to the loss of religion. A similar confusion and loss would attend the demand of one who should require an Either-Or choice between all that Christianity stands for and all that Buddhism stands for.

In the years of its early vigour, Christianity was vigorously syncretistic.* It was also highly intolerant,

* It is unnecessary to retrace here the well-known outline of these adoptions from the language and thought of the Greco-Roman world, from the philosophies and from the mysteries. What Christianity has done in the way of absorbing ceremonial observances, of adopting dates for Christmas and

in the sense that it was unwilling to compromise or to adulterate its worship with any element it deemed inconsistent therewith. Christian and Jew alike refused to worship the Emperor: syncretism involved no acceptance of other gods. Christians refused to deny what they did worship, even to save their own lives: syncretism had no tendency to promote such denial. Christianity kept its entire sternness in the denunciation of abuses in the religion around it: the recognition of some of their elements as valuable, so far from impeding this denunciation, actually facilitated it. This indicates that syncretism and a sound intolerance are not incompatible with each other. We need not deprive ourselves of a new glimpse of truth in order to retain the virtue of a virile intolerance.

Our conclusion in regard to this method is first of all that there is something not alone valid but necessary in the process of Synthesis. There is a spiritual life of Asia which has not alone to be conserved but learned from. There can be only one situation in which two religions in contact have no occasions for synthesis, namely, when one of the two contains all that the other has, and something over. This is certainly not the case in any Asiatic contact. Hence I venture to propose that no *religion can become a religion for Asia which does not fuse the spiritual genius of Asia with that of Western Christianity;* and not alone the genius of Asia, but that of each of its major great religions.

Easter, is of minor importance. But these appropriations have been successful in the sense that they have become organic parts of the Christian totality; they have so domesticated themselves as to leave no joint to make one conscious that "This is an accretion."

For Christianity there must be a more open attitude, in particular to the local religions. It is not in the same relation of rivalry towards them as towards the other universal religions. Unless it is prepared to assume the cultural load carried by these traditions it has no occasion nor right to proclaim war against them. It has especial need, if it cannot adopt the relation of double-belonging which Buddhism has found possible in China, Japan, India, at least to preserve in its own body what it can of their local meaning.* Its actual course has been the opposite. It has especially attacked, and tried to supplant the local faiths; it has identified them with their more superstitious popular aspects; it has neglected to challenge the universal aspects of religion with anything like the same directness and vigour. It has thus failed to make adequate use of the chief sources from which it could derive an added strength.

In the fear of syncretism, we have a justified, but on the whole timorous attitude to alien religions: it shows a smallness of faith in what one has which, at every point, tends to deprive of sustenance that very religion which it seeks so sedulously to preserve. For, it must be repeated, these new ingredients *belong* to it. They are lacking to it now by our inadequacy, not its own; by what right do we seek to hedge it off from its rightful stature?

Why, for example, when we consider that the terms

*Double-belonging has possibilities which are being explored from the side of the local religions rather than from the side of Christianity: for example, the "Indian Followers of Christ." The responsible organisation of the Church makes the exploration from the Christian side difficult—it cannot be called impossible.

of other languages alter the original meanings of the Hebrew terms, do we assume that the deviation corrupts rather than enriches? Why has a translator no confidence that a total spirit will impress itself upon words, giving them its own colour, though a new one to that word? If meaning is alive, it always moulds its own vessels.

I believe that we shall see in the Orient the rise of a Christianity far outpassing that which we of the West have conceived, simply because it can recover there so many lost fragments of what is its own. Our western religion has gone literal, through much struggle with a literal-minded race: religion advances out of the poetic and imaginative towards the literal, and where there is still poetry, the springs of religion are still young. And in those springs we may well meet in their original freshness some of the ancient, eternal sources of our faith.

> I often think of what C. F. Andrews said on one occasion in answer to a crudely direct question of mine— whether he had been engaged in trying to convert Indians to Christianity. He looked at me with a glance in which I thought I detected an element of rebuke as well as of surprise. "I always assume," he said, "that they *are* Christians; and after I have talked with them for a while I sometimes see the light of Christ coming into their eyes." My first impulse was to ask by what right Andrews assumed that the Indians are already Christians; my later impulse is to ask by what right we assume that they are not. Is it to be assumed that Christ's presence in Asia has waited the arrival of our ships and our Bibles? John's Gospel contradicts such an assumption.

But there are certain remarks to be made about this way of Synthesis:

It is less a policy than *something which happens to you* whenever minds are open and unafraid or simply unguarded. Conversation is normally an exchange of ideas; learning is normally always bilateral: it requires resolution, not to grow, but to resist growth. What one admires in the world of ideas one has already appropriated.* The more there is of life in an idea, the more it seems ready to attract other ideas. Wherever there is a premonition of fertility, ideas reach out in an endless and various polygamy, to develop beyond what their own unpaired germ would yield. This appropriation of kin-germinals is always going on.

It is *always mutual*. On the whole, in Asia, up to the present it is chiefly the non-Christian religions which have developed in this way, by taking over some aspects of Christianity. This process, looked at as an (unintended) effect of the presence of Christianity is sometimes referred to as "permeation"; and by the Christian authorities is partly welcomed and partly feared as if the borrowing were a theft. But it cannot be much affected by either hopes or fears; since it is far less a deliberate activity of competitive imitation than a spontaneous adoption.

* And where there is overt conflict and rivalry, there is likely to be, as an accompaniment of the vocal criticism of the opposing system, a movement of inner reform in the direction of the strengths of that system. Thus, the invasion of India by Islam influenced the direction of reform movements in Hinduism, if not those movements themselves. Kabir, Guru Nanak, Ramananda were certainly guided by what they saw in Islam. And it is possible that Sankara and Ramanuja were also influenced by Islam. Cf. Tara Chand, *Influence of Islam on Indian Culture*, Allahabad, 1936.

It is *not adequate*. Clearly it is one of those processes which leads to the convergence of different religions, without solving the issues between them. Further, it is not a complete operation; it is but the assembling stage preliminary to a further process of thought. We turn to a third way.

3

THE WAY OF RECONCEPTION

In the natural order of experience, broadening is preliminary to deepening.

The first business of childhood is the accumulation of riches—wide collection of facts, names, ideas, with no particular concern for their order or their nature. The stage of insight which we call "understanding" follows slowly; the ambition to master things by penetrating their "nature" arrives with maturity.

The religious experience of the race follows a similar pattern. The many gods of the early world belong to the stage of accumulation: they are records of the wide variety of primitive religious experience, care-free in respect to order, careful only for the faithful preservation of every inkling of the divine. They are preparations for that stage of "understanding" which discerns that the many gods are one. This rhythm of broadening and deepening recurs. In the later world, when the several great systems of faith are brought, as now, into intimate contact, there is a new era of broadening, in which each religion extends its base to comprise what it finds valid in other strands of tradition. But this also must serve as preliminary to that deepening which is a search for better grasp of its own essence.

For broadening necessarily stimulates the deepening process. One's conceptions have been inadequate; they have not anticipated these new vistas and motives:

we require to understand our own religion better—
we must *reconceive it*—then we shall see how the new
perspectives belong quite naturally to what has always
been present in its nature, unnoticed or unappreciated
by us.

We are at the dawn of this new stage of deepening.
In the contemporary epoch, in which the position and
meaning of religion are in constant question, inclu-
siveness in the content of faith becomes a secondary
aim. All the sails of the mind have for some time been
set for exploration and acquisition; there are really
few who need any longer to be admonished not to
reject what is good in what to them is foreign. The
great effort now required is the effort to discern the
substance of the matter underlying all this profusion
of religious expression, to apprehend the generating
principle of religious life and of each particular form
of it.

The word "essence" refers to this generating principle, the single germ from which the many expressions
are derived and can therefore be understood. As every
living thing has its germ-cell-group*, so has every
project, undertaking, institution, historical movement
its essence. This essence can easily be ungrasped or
misunderstood; and if a leader or statesman misappre-

---

* The organic analogy is fairly precise, even to its tantalising ambi-
guities. We cannot understand the oak from the acorn without also understanding the acorn from the oak; growth is no mere unpacking of a magic
parcel in which every subsequent development is precontained, it is the
appropriation of novelty and adventure, it is also creation; the germ is but
the opportunity upon which time gathers its undreamed-of spoils; hence all
this reading backward into the germ of what has developed is subject to
illusion. Nevertheless, there is a germ, which is the core of identity; and we
keep learning about it from the very novelties which it has made possible.

hends the essence of his business, fails to know what can be thrown overboard in storm and what must on no account be surrendered, he heads for disaster. To know the essence of a religion is peculiarly difficult (as the succession of early church councils may witness). It is always a matter of degree and an unfinished enterprise, so that we must now and again return to it. In proportion as we grasp it, we can distinguish what is indispensable from what is relatively accidental and variable. To possess the essence would be to have sureness, and therefore freedom and courage, in recognising truth wherever there is truth, as well as in rejecting encumbrances, retained antiquities, excess, pretence, accretion. It would be to give to our impulsive sympathy the discriminating power of unerring instinct.

How is the essence to be found? Not by comparison, nor by analysis—though these help: it is found by what the logician calls "induction," namely a *perception of the reason* why a given group of facts or experiences do belong together. For this perception (which is often the work of genius) no rules can be given; it comes as a discovery, an illumination. "Induction" is but a word which covers the uncommandable insight; induction is the discovery of essence.

But the broadening of the base of experience aids in discerning the essence. For it is just these anticipatory warmings of the mind toward what is felt to be kindred in other faiths which begin to release us from bondage to the accidental in our own.

One day I was visiting, with a companion of unimpeachable orthodoxy, the temple of the Sleeping Buddha near Colombo. A woman was praying, not at the immense recumbent image of the Buddha, but at a small standing image at its feet. We questioned the attendant priest. "Do you not pray to the Buddha?" "No; the Buddha has entered Nirvana; he is no longer concerned with the affairs on this earth." "To whom do you pray?" "To the Bodhisattvas. This standing image represents a Bodhisattva. He is now in the Universe, and will some day come to the earth to renew the knowledge of the truth, which men are always forgetting." "Does that coming of the Bodhisattva mean anything to you?" asked my companion. "O yes. When he comes, there will be an end of war and hatred; there will be a time of peace and kindness. I hope for his coming. I long for his coming!" There was fervour in the answer. To my surprise, my orthodox companion said, "I join in your hope!" He had swiftly accepted, across wide differences of concepts and imagery, an identity of meaning: to this extent he was coming upon the essence of a symbol common to the two faiths.

The intimations of Synthesis are the natural preparation for Reconception. And the deepenings of Reconception render Synthesis less a separate process than a spontaneous movement of life.

The relation between the three methods may be clarified by a figure—the diagram being, as Whitehead says, the modern form of the Platonic myth!

The way of Reconception has its own dangers. It may be supposed that the essence is sufficient. In that case the search for essence might be a reduction of religion to bare bones, and a discarding of everything but the centre. If the essence seems to present itself as a small group of general principles, the particular aspects of religion are especially likely to be taken as extraneous, and one reverts to religion-in-general.

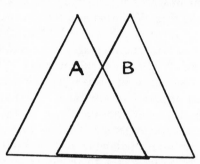

Two religions, A and B, are represented as being partly coincident or overlapping in their present teaching and character. The subsequent diagrams will represent the three ways to a world faith which we have now discussed, as practised by A—religion B being assumed for simplicity's sake to remain passive.

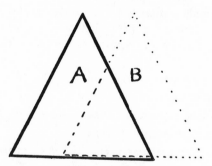

1. Radical Displacement

A hardens its own outline, excluding all of B except what is now included in A

This is an obvious misuse of the method. To find the life which runs to the various members is not to cancel the members. To find the law which describes the growth of a tree is not to cancel the tree. To discover the premiss from which conclusions follow is not to escape the conclusions; on the contrary, it is to keep those conclusions, to possess them more per-

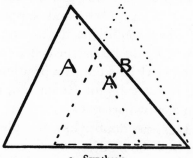

2. Synthesis

A reaches over to include what it finds valid in B, but with some distortion in its own shape.

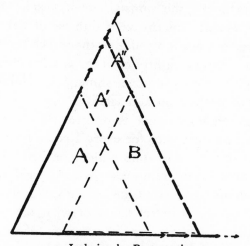

3. Inclusion by Reconception

The apex of the cone A, its conceived essence, moves upward, until without distortion the cone A includes what is valid of B, and indefinitely more, as self-understanding deepens.

fectly. To perceive in any measure the essence of a religion is to be more rather than less alive to all of its functions, and to all its implications.

With this warning, the way of Reconception is peculiarly fitted to meet the groping of an age which, with a certain prevalent dulness, doubts whether it can have any religion at all; and supposing that it can set up its own conditions for accepting religion, requires it not alone to be useful and intelligible, but above all to be brief! It is not in a position to perform an Induction, but it calls for Reduction, and inclines to assume that the two are one.

Such demands, no doubt, like the philistine's demands on art, lack the modesty which would be appropriate to dulness; they forget that the only God whom man can use is a God who makes demands on *him*. Nevertheless, the human demand also has its place in God's world; and the very dulness of the cry for Reduction may act as a guide in the search for essence. What the demand rightly calls for is what this search may supply—not an impoverishment of religion, but a recovery of proportion and vitality.

The search for essence is progressive. It comes to no final stopping place; for every Reconception, there is conceivably a better one still to be had.* It is the natural process of religious growth, because it is growth *within sameness*; each new discernment of the "essence" is but a better sense of what has all along been seen and taught; it is a new grasp of the eternal identity of the faith.

It thus escapes the fallacy of that Modernism which insisted on the relativity of all stages of religious teaching, and failed to see that religion in its nature

* It is in this respect akin to the process of Interpretation as defined by Royce. Cf. *Problem of Christianity*, vol. ii, p. 149 f.

must unite men with the everlasting and changeless.* The change is in our apprehension; we can hardly pretend that this our finite apprehension needs no improvement!† All our judgments of the essence of Christianity contain an element of certainty, and also of uncertainty—an ingredient of hypothesis. On account of this factor of uncertainty, there is a call from time to time for further induction based on wider groups of fact and on better insight into their nature.

The succession of such hypotheses—since each supplies a lack in the preceding—constitutes a consecutive argument, or development; it is the "dialectic" of religious insight in the legitimate meaning of that

* There is something inexorable about the truth; it is not what it is because of any one's wishes. It is the Rock; and because of this, the primary need of the heart for finality, there is the recurrent appeal to Revelation and to its attribute, Authority. The Christian Church asserts this authority: it has the truth: *Sit ut est aut non sit.*

The difficulty has been to admit growth into what is final. We must have both. When any person or group adopts the position insisting exclusively on finality, we immediately become conscious of the human element with all its trivialities and self-importances intruding upon the legitimate ideal. Whenever, on the other hand, the Modernist insists on the human element, with its implications of the possibilities of change and growth, the uneasy spectre of flabbiness, desertion of the central citadel of finality, appears. Neither profession alone is tolerable..

The solution lies in these experiences themselves. Something is final in what I have; but not all that I have is final. It is the drawing of this invisible line that is required. This cannot be done by geometry: it requires a process of distillation, repeated distillation, which gradually reveals the essence of unchangeable validity which from the beginning has been the strength of the mixture.

† It is peculiar to Christianity that in its view revelation is progressive and unfinished: this is one of the meanings of the doctrine of the Holy Spirit, the perpetual contemporaneousness, personalness, and novelty of the unfolding of the meaning of its truth. No one who declines to admit that form of change which means the arrival of new light—"He shall guide you into all truth"—has understood this doctrine.

word. For "dialectic" may be defined as consecutive induction.*

In proportion as any religion grows in self-understanding through grasping its own essence, it grasps the essence of all religion, and gains in *power to interpret* its various forms.

To interpret is the best gift which one religion can bring to another. Power to interpret is the power to say more truly or in more understandable language what an idea or a usage "means"; to interpret is to give a voice to what is relatively inarticulate and defenceless. It is indeed to some extent to improve and alter, in so far as it separates the chaff from the wheat; but it does keep the wheat and bring it to market. The interpreter is able to save a great deal which the honest but rude excluder feels impelled to throw away.

In this sense, Reconception is the way of a *true conservatism:* it conserves as much as possible of what is worth conserving in other faiths; it provides a permanent frame for all those scattered "accents of the Holy Ghost" which, treasured in local traditions here and there, are robbed by their separateness of their due force.

There is, one feels, a certain *noblesse oblige* in the relations among religions; those who have travelled far in the path of self-understanding have an obligation to those less skilled in self-explanation. Instead of using this advantage to beat their opponents down, it

* This notion of the empirical dialectic is to be distinguished from the pseudo-deductive dialectic of Hegel, as well as from the experimental pragmatism of Dewey; it is, I suggest, the union of their valid elements.

becomes a matter of chivalry to express for them their meanings better than they themselves could express them. The joy of refutation is a poor and cheap-bought joy in comparison with the joy of lifting a struggling thought to a new level of self-understanding.

Thus, instead of attempting to shut other religions up in metaphysical compartments, and then destroying the compartments, it would certainly be fairer—not to say more honourable—if we were to attempt rather to anticipate for them what they mean, opening to them that larger room toward which they trend.

Let us suppose, for example, that the cult of ancestors in China leans too much towards a "worship" of the finite, and to a dependence on some magical exchange with them for family fortune. The point to which we have to attend is that the family bond is a normal part of religion in any community; that it has a reasonable place in ritual; that it need not be superstitious; that it requires to be made elastic and compatible with regard for the new national spirit; but that it ought on no account to be expunged.

> Homer Ling, civil engineer in the Public Works Dept. of Amoy, a graduate of Massachusetts Institute of Technology, is a third generation Christian. He provided the city of Amoy and the International Settlement on an adjacent island with its new water supply, an admirable piece of engineering. His grandfather was obliged on becoming a Christian to destroy his ancestral tablets. He himself was planning (1932) to build in Amoy an ancestral hall for his clan, in the belief that the cult of ancestors is not inherently inconsistent with Christianity, and that China requires for its new life a renewed hold on the moral bonds of the family which the changing conditions tend to dissolve.

Or if the Buddhist doctrine of the Void appears to us what it literally professes to be, a worship of nothing at all, the most empty and meaningless, the most dehumanising of all objects of faith, we are surely bound to look beyond the letter; and to interpret the baffling words in terms of the Ineffable of all mysticism, the "Gott ist ein lauter Nichts" of Silesius, or the "stille Wüste der Gottheit" of Eckhart—vehement rejections of the applicability of our qualities or our idea of "thing" to the being of the Absolute. For us, too, the real is no "thing."

The principle is that the ideas of others, like all living entities, must be given the benefit of their direction. They are presumably in partial error. If so, we always have the choice between two comments: either "You are on the wrong track"; or else "*This is what you are trying for.*" The latter remark calls for a far severer labour of thought. It cannot be made solely on the basis of a dogma faithfully held. "Whom therefore ye ignorantly worship, him declare I unto you" is not the remark of a mind bringing forward a settled formula. It is the remark of one who has paid in terms of contemporary observation and new thinking the high cost of the power to interpret.

How does this method make for a world faith?

Evidently, if one and only one religion could succeed in absorbing into its own essence the meaning of all the others, that religion would attract the free suffrage of mankind to itself. Any such result would necessarily be remote, since the essence cannot be taken by storm; light upon its nature will appear only gradually, and through the slow intimations of meaning as intuitive understanding of the expressions of other faiths is increased. The specific social and historical functions of the local religions could in their nature never be completely replaced by the essence of a universal religion; a truly universal religion would provide a place for such local functions.

But, as Synthesis is mutual, so is Reconception. All religions in contact with one another will be spurred to this kind of deepened self-understanding. At present, in the Far East, Buddhism, Christianity, Hinduism driven by the intense cultural self-consciousness of the historical moment, are all attempting to restate their own essences, and so to state them as to include what they regard as significant in the others. This makes again for a growing resemblance among religions—that is, among the conceptions of the essence of Buddhism, Christianity, Hinduism, that emerge.* And there is certainly no immediate tendency to diminish the number of particular religions.

Nevertheless, the process *does tend to a decision*, not through a conflict of faiths or a campaign for world dominance, but through the unforced persuasiveness of relative success in this effort to become a better vehicle of truth.

The notion of competition among religions is in-

* Rev. C. Burnell Olds, of Okayama, found that all groups consulted by him in Japan were prepared to agree that the essence of religion is love— love as the basis of the universe and as the root of human righteousness. In this formulation, however, the essence of *religion* is in the foreground, whereas our present concern is with the particular essences of the several religions—the essence of Christianity, etc.

An account of one phase of Mr. Olds' "Venture in Understanding" in Okayama is reprinted in an appendix, p. 273.

trinsically distasteful: competition to displace is precisely that element of discord which the statesman
finds most repulsive in the religious scene. But there
is an aspect of competition which is right and endurable
—a competition to understand and include, a rivalry
as to which religion can best express the meaning of
the rest; which can save most of the religious treasury
of the race—such a rivalry can hardly beget antagonism.

Nor could it be a misfortune for the race if the
several living religions should find themselves spurred
in one another's presence to such a rivalry. When all
religions are losing their hold on multitudes, no one
can say that any of them is doing too well, through its
human representatives, what a religion has to do for
the soul of man! They are all wretched vessels. They
are all wrapped in sanctimony, dusty-eyed with self-
satisfaction, stiff-jointed with the rheum-rust of their
creedal conceits, so timorous under the whips of
conformity that only a few dare the perilous task of
thinking, and the complacency-disturbing task of
trying the spirit of other faiths. They wear the aspect
of senility, while the world is crying to them to be
young; they can no longer take a true creed in their
lips, and have it carry the meaning of truth, since the
blood, life, passion are gone out of it, and it has become
a festoon of dried husks. Men are not unready for
faith, even for concrete and particular faith, if they can
find life in it. These are their questions:

Which religion, in its account of the need and lostness of the human heart, can get farthest beyond
platitudes and mere general lament, into the region of
the literal struggle of human life with evil, sordidness,

and that blight of meaninglessness which besets human success no less than human failure. Which one most truly diagnoses the root of the malady? Which one provides a positive meaning for life without relying on a tinselled and sugared otherworldliness on one hand, nor falling, on the other, into the cant of "timeless values"?

Which religion does in fact most verifiably save men from greed, lust, and hatred, and without destroying their virility and effectiveness as members of race and social order? Which is most proof against hypocrisy, duplicity and pretence?* Which confers most genuine zest for dangerous and principled living, releases positive moral power, abets a single-mindedness which can discount accident, hostility, and failure? Which one develops greatness without narrowness, and conviction without servility. Which one begets prophets who can get the ear of the godless, sophisticated, intelligent, sagacious, and critical, as well as the ear of the suggestible, dependent, sentimental, or committed?

Which religion is most fertile? Which best sustains that metaphysical urge which is the life of the arts, of great and new poetry, drama, architecture, music?

* President Lim, Confucianist, knew that the deacons of a certain Christian church in Amoy were engaged in a lucrative trade of smuggling liquor into the Settlement. He confronted some of them with this knowledge, saying: "Why do you do this? If your own doctrines are true, you will go to Hell." And me he confronted with the question, "Why does Christianity not touch the conscience? Confucianism does!"

This was, I presume, partly by way of a *tu quoque*, in view of the usual western conception of Confucianism as a cult of external propriety without sincerity. But few of us realise to what an extent since the war of 1914 the feeling has spread in the Orient that Christianity is a religion recommended to others, not seriously entertained by its professors.

A true religion invites cosmic courage, including the belief that the human mind is called upon to know its universe—not to find its equation, but by degrees to understand it. It is not cowed by the spectacle of infinity; it is freed to see meanings in things, to play with traditional ideas, as Dante, Milton, Bunyan played, setting other men free from literalism and the planetary provincialisms of the human outlook. The order of culture is religion, art, philosophy—religion being the fruitful centre, when it is alive.

Which religion is most fertile in men? Which sends into the life of the state those convinced and solitary persons who give what no society could ever require of them or even define, and yet without which any society dies of anæmia?

And which religion, while thus serving the public life of its time can best retain its own proud authority? Which best escapes being harnessed to nostrums and "movements," while evaluating them as they come and go? Which resists being drawn excitedly into the great social programme of the moment through a self-betraying dread that it may lose its "leadership"? Which refrains with greatest inner stability from crying up its wares when the world goes awry, as if its value suddenly rose with general panic and disaster? Which best retains, and confers, amid its ferments, incitements, and ovulations, the serenity of the eternal and the all-embracing peace of God?

When the religions realise that these are the questions which they must eventually meet, and that no charter from the Most High God will excuse them from meeting them, nor give them any dominion on the earth if they do not, the search for their own essence may become, as it is due to be, a grave and anxious search rather than any mere exercise of scholarly speculation.

This process needs a new institution. Though Reconception is always going on, wherever religious self-consciousness is alive, it requires in the present world-period for its favourable pursuit an institution widely different from the usual type of Protestant mission—not to supplant that mission but to supplement it.

The mission is set for teaching; the required institution must be set for learning as well. The mission is set for the announcement of doctrine; this institution must be set as well for conversation and conference. The mission is set for activity; this institution must be set also for leisure, contemplation, study. The mission is set for address to its own region; this institution must be set for give and take with the thought and feeling of a nation and a world.

The essential parts of such an institution are, beside the quarters for living and hospitality, the library, the facilities for conference, meditation, worship, the good will of the religious leadership of all groups in the region, access to natural solitude and to the life of city and country.

And prior to all this, or perhaps connected with it as a training place, a school for the higher study of the thought, art and literature of the surrounding culture.

What is required is a watch-tower of thought and understanding, in which the chief activity is not the building of the church but the activity of the reflective observer, qualified by a deep knowledge of the spiritual backgrounds of the life around him, prepared to meet its best thought on its own ground, and sensitive to the movements of change always present in that life. For the Protestant missions, this function, essential to any vital progress in meeting the new Orient, is an almost vacant function. The Roman Catholic missions are better provided.

At Kurseong, about eight miles southward of Darjeeling, there is St. Mary's, a university for the final studies of Jesuit missionaries. Every Jesuit who is to work in India goes first, after perhaps two years of college study in his own country, to an institution in Southern India, where he receives four years of "philosophical training." He learns here something of the sciences and philosophies of the West, but also something of the languages, literatures, and religions of India. After this, he spends three years as apprentice to some existing mission, or makes his own studies among the Indian people. A young friend of mine from St. Louis had spent these years on the Indian road; with his bedding-roll on his back, he had gone through the countryside, stopping in villages, eating, drinking, living with villagers, incidentally taking some of their diseases, coming through alive and with an intimate knowledge of some phases of Indian life, as well as a command of one or two dialects. Following this apprenticeship, there are the final three or four years at St. Mary's, the "theological training." This includes, beside study of theology and philosophy of the West, further study of the religious classics of India. The library is well stocked with these books. Not until these ten to eleven years of training are finished can a Jesuit act as a missionary in his own right. He is usually in his early thirties when this course is completed. And with what result? This at least: that

wherever you meet a Jesuit missionary in India, you meet
a man of culture, of broad sympathy, who has taken the
trouble to know the deeper phases and sources of the life
around him. While in Darjeeling, I wished to visit a
Tibetan monastery. But I had no way of access, nor could
I gain any information about its personnel and activities
until I met a Father Wright, English Jesuit, who told me
about its library, the monks who were philosophically
interested, with whom I could converse. The men who
come out from St. Mary's are a group of strongly equipped
spirits, reflecting competently on the whole range of the
cultural problems of India, and of its connections. I think
of them as a sort of wing over Asia, poised, unhurried,
with firm judgment and far vision, putting the strength of
their insight at the service of the work of the Church, and
ready to converse with the traveller who has similar
concerns. In comparison with this, our Protestant institutions are set for prompt delivery of partly prepared men.
It is as though the graduate level of adept preparation were
out of tune with our sense of haste and scantiness of
means. Yet the resources of the Protestant societies are in
general beyond those of the Catholic societies; and certainly in the aggregate, far greater. The real lack, among
Protestants, is a lack of perception; a certain triviality and
crudity in the sense of the work to be done; a supposition that we already know enough, and that more
thinking is a luxury that can be dispensed with. In
my judgment, this pioneering shack-built conception
of the mission has had its day; and whatever notable
achievements lie before the mission of the future
are to be the reward of depth of competence rather
than of the attempt to *cover the ground* with a super-
ficial propaganda.

In respect to the stern conditions of the work of
understanding we have much to learn from such a
foundation as St. Mary's. But there are as yet no
institutions, Protestant or Catholic, which have the

aim and amplitude of the institution here proposed.* Germs of such an enterprise do indeed exist here and there, which indicate that the need is making itself felt. And in time, I foresee a chain of such centres set around the world, hospitable to qualified enquirers, and contributing—as centres of art contribute to the life of art—to sustain the continuing enterprise of reconceiving religion through world culture, and world culture through religion.

* In its conception there is some analogy in the ashram of Tagore at Santiniketan, where Hindu, Christian, Moslem, Buddhist find themselves at home, and where creative work in several of the fine arts adds itself to scholarship, worship, social experiment, to bring to a single focus the new and the old life of Asia.

LECTURE IV

THE PRESENT STAGE
AND THE NEXT

THE PRESENT STAGE AND THE NEXT

W E have reviewed the major processes making for a world faith. Some of them, like the mission, are deliberately so aimed; some of them are undeliberate like the tides of conviction underlying the contemporary outlook; some of them, like the momentous influences of political authority, barely touched upon in our discussion, are partly deliberate and partly undeliberate. Do these numerous processes conspire to any net and readable result at this moment of world history?

As for the deliberate efforts, such as we have just now been considering, the total achievement hardly bears the look of a consensus. All deliberate propaganda has a measure of success—it finds its own. And because it all succeeds, it all fails to make any faith exclusive. Each active religion gets some hearing everywhere; the domains of these religions interpenetrate.

Even the local religions develop distillates which expand rapidly. Hinduism in the form of Rama-krishna-Vedantism pervades the world; in a more popular form, it spreads eastward.* Shinto under refined guises sends missions to Asia and America. And though Islam remains strongly localised, yet

* On April 25, 1937 the Bengal Hindu Mission, Calcutta, "decided to send an overseas mission for the propagation of Hinduism in the eastern countries, including Java, Bali, Indo-China, Siam, China and Japan. . . . The Mission also decided to open a College of Religion at Benares. (It) will give instruction in the comparative study of religion and the history of the missionary propaganda of the different religions of the world."—*The Guardian*, Madras, April 29, 1937, p. 270.

through the diaphanous medium of Bahaism it moves anonymously and swiftly into attuned circles which might find the Koran difficult.

And wherever any faith has all-but-exclusive prevalence there is always at least one other, Judaism, borne not by converts but by its own people voluntarily or involuntarily scattered. Firm in its distinctive qualities and prepared through its unobtrusive presence, its rapid numerical increase,* and the inherent rationality and realism of its simple creed, to commend itself when the more pretentious claimants by their very complexity fail any longer to convince, it waits to inherit the earth spiritually as residuary legatee. It conceives itself as the ultimate world faith, not through the effort of man but by the act of God.

Thus the missions intercross and the map of world religion becomes for the present intricate and entangled. Nevertheless, there is a certain growth of agreement; for the would-be persuader is always to some extent persuaded. The adaptation of his message to the perception of his hearers is also an adoption of something of theirs—a subtle Synthesis. The Moslem mission to England at Woking, Surrey, has its own version of Islam, of which the unbiased reader must judge that the effort to commend it to Englishmen has drawn it in the direction of the ethos of Christendom.†
The stronger convictions of mankind bend the weaker ones to themselves through the very process intended to supplant them.

* The Jewish population of the world has doubled since 1880.

† The word Islam is said, in the official journal of this mission, to mean 'peace'; Islam is accordingly the religion of peace *par excellence*. It is also distinguished for the high position which it accords to women, etc.

The undeliberate changes (as we have seen) make for a measure of common mind within the several religions, without turning the scales toward any one of them.*

Perhaps we may say that they tend to develop a certain acceptance of religious variety; not by dropping the postulate that religion must be universal, but by an increased sympathy with the growing-pains of religious change, and a deepened appreciation of the preciousness of the local roots. The world appears to have become more understanding of the unique nature of religious insight, with its gentler and freer sort of exploring, its greater natural play for subjective and imaginative variety, whose aberrations are to be reduced—not by the sledge-hammer decisiveness of the experimental testing which physical science can use, but by gradual give and take with regional social experience. Mankind is not clear that it would benefit if all the poetry of prophecy were at once limited to a single source. It is more content to feel that the desired unity is arriving, unwritten and unimposed, like the silent filling of a reservoir among the hills, taking its gradual contribution from diverse human tentatives, to be protected in their shrinking from intrusion. In this respect, the historical sense of the race seems to me to be growing more like the loving-kindness of God.

We must ourselves give attention to this reservoir, whose level perceptibly rises. What is happening may be considered as a vast process of racial thinking. It makes the great religions more alike. But at the same time—not less important—it brings the unreligious

* Lecture II, p. 116 above.

and anti-religious groups nearer to these classified as religious. Especially the wavering and critical groups, prisoners of the scruples begotten by scientific conscience, begin to see the meaning of religion in a highly cautious and general but natural fashion. It is possible, I think, to perceive the touch of a new *rapprochement*. As we put off the discreditable fears begotten by the conception of the Only Way, our eyes are opened for the recognition of identities of meaning under different guises. We are able to see that the ingredients of a world-faith are present, far more widespread and substantial than we have commonly imagined.

EMERGING ELEMENTS OF WORLD FAITH

THERE is a prevalent trait of our time which facilitates its approach to religion. This trait is usually expressed by saying that our age is "psychological"; it is skilled in observing its own states. It naturally begins its world view with "experience" regarding experience as in some sense "inner," that is, as belonging to the self. So far as experience is "mine"—all sensations are "my" sensations, all events are "my" events, eliciting my feelings and responses—I am sure of it. Our time is at home in this position of nuclear security, and from this position moves outward towards its objects.

Thus in regard to religion, our time is more disposed to recognise it as a normal aspect of human nature than to adopt any item of an objective creed: there is much religiousness abroad which gets no farther than a belief in religion! It understands that religion belongs to the realm of feeling. It is not indisposed to consider religion as a passion for righteousness and its spread, somehow differentiated from morality by the feeling of obligation that accompanies it. It does not begin with a belief in God but with a religious faith in duty. It cautiously moves on from this point to consider what is implied; and this minimal, exploring religiousness is the groundwork for those elements of world faith which appear to me to be emerging very generally among mankind, because they are the natural inferences from this point of beginning.

It is becoming slowly recognised that where obligation or duty exists, there must be some object fit for that feeling: there can be no obligation to the lifeless, nor to the inanimate, nor to the morally blind. If the cosmos conveys to me a sense of moral demand, the term "God" begins to acquire a core of meaning no longer repellent to the scientific consciousness. Enlightened mankind is far less disposed now than even a score of years ago to boggle over the word "God," since it sees the way to reticent conceptions of God, such as those of Confucius or of the supposed atheist Buddha.

The experimental atheism of the last quarter of a century has done much service in this direction: it is running through the course of its own argument, and making the ancient discovery along new lines. Atheism as a rule is a denial not of God but of some reputed conception of God, more or less fallacious; such atheisms are therefore partly true. But the negative posture is strained and cannot long remain satisfying: one denies only on the basis of some affirmation. The contemporary materialisms, like that of the Stoics, tend to show themselves crusts which conceal a living fire.*

Righteousness, we say, is felt to be a cosmic demand. Is the cosmos then good? Is it possible that the con-

---

* The "dialectical materialism" of certain Marxian schools in Moscow interprets matter as "autodynamic"—as self-moving or spontaneous. Organisms manifest in their actions the initiative which pertains to the material elements. This is to read life back into matter, and so to denature materialism.

temporary mind is ready to accept any such implication about the world it faces?

The official dogma to the effect that "God is good" is contradicted to the eye of common observation by the sufferings of the entire animated universe. Buddha was free to dwell on suffering, for he had no God whose goodness he felt bound to uphold. The attempt to bolster the dogma of goodness by weighing pleasures against pains can never lead to more than a dubious result; to such efforts to plaster the attribute of goodness upon a God first found as a factual object our era is perhaps more disinclined than any previous era in history. If life is not good, God is not good; and we would better avoid the word God, as did original Buddhism. But must we judge whether life is good or not by looking at these spot-contents of experience with their motley mixtures of joy and grief, elevation, drabness, wretchedness, whose balance is forever indecisive and unfinished? The truth is, we wait for no such scale-tipping. We judge life on the basis of something far more immediate and nuclear, the satisfaction of being alive. In the primitive fact of *being conscious* there is a satisfaction independent of the contents of consciousness. To exist, as being aware of things, able to perceive and judge—this is to enjoy existence. Any spot of experience whatever—pleasant, painful, indifferent—is to this extent an enjoyed spot.

This primitive self-enjoyment constitutes what we may call our aboriginal value-prejudice. Experience is loaded in advance on the side of good; living and the love of living are inseparable, and this prejudice extends to the world as the source of living.

The problem of evil is not solved by this prejudice: it is made by it. Because life is good, evil becomes a "problem" as good does not. We take pain as a stimulus, not as a ledger item of value.* All apparent spot-values are provisional—especially the negative values.

This is peculiarly true of the ingredient of pain which lurks in the centre of awareness itself; for living is a sort of destruction, a burning of tissue and a consuming of energy. Buddha may have been reporting an experience of intensely focussed introspection when he declared: "Life is suffering, life is a burning." But if so, he was too much the psychologist, subject to the illusion of the artificial quiescence he had forced upon himself in the interest of meditation. Life as an active moving-on has a different report to make of its value. As active, life is still a burning, even more a burning; but it is also struggle. And struggle, which brings its own type of pain with it, brings also enhanced being; and this enhanced being is capable of so heightening self-enjoyment as to render the involved pain negligible.†

The ultimate source of good stands above the struggle. We know intuitively not alone that the joy of action may discount all included pain, but that beyond action the wakening of the mind to love and the opening

* If a painful stimulus arrives, we retract our sense-organs; it does not naturally occur to us to escape the pain by obliterating consciousness.

† This is the strength and the weakness of the Nietzsches and Hitlers; their glorification of combat has an astringent corrective quality, as compared with the laments of passive burning. But fighting per se is a muddled and confused value-region, good not in itself, but only by borrowing from the sense of being, which holds its own in non-exertion as in exertion.

of the eyes to beauty are the essence of happiness; and in their presence no other qualities of experience carry weight. This is the element of insight in the Indian conception of Nirvana; only, Nirvana is carried along with us in the nuclear experience of struggle as well as of peace, and requires the experience of struggle to elicit its meaning.

If life is evil, extinction is a benefit; if life is good, death becomes an evil, and we beat against the limit which it marks to our being. On the immortality of the self there is no emerging element of faith; but there is a widespread disposition to reopen the question, in view of a new perception of its meaning.

The abuses of otherworldliness have been the chief source of hostility to religion. The doctrine of survival of death has provided the occasion for most of the excesses of supernaturalism, the invitation for grotesque extravagance in the fancies of good and evil destiny, the locus of the High Court of ultimate judgment and reward, the pivot of all the illicit pressures of instituted pretence playing upon the fears and hopes of the credulous masses of mankind, hence the nursery of spurious powers against which the State and all rational social effort have to contend. As wholly unverifiable, assertions about the other world and the other life are the special object of pragmatic-positivistic detestation; and the *bête noire* of the humanistic realists, communist or other, who would spur man on to save himself and to do it in this world while we are still here to enjoy the results! If there is anything on which we might claim emerging agreement among men, it might seem to be the rejection of interest in "immortality" as not merely irrelevant but inimical to the serious business of mankind. Yet here again a different view of things makes a swift passage into general judgment.

Prior to all the abuses of supernaturalism, and therefore free from them, there is an elemental conviction which arises in this same region of nuclear self-consciousness. It is the conviction that values do not survive the subjects which perceive them. If, then, there are any true values as distinct from the tinsel and deception of the spot-values of experience, *the subject of such true values ought not to perish.* It is mere rhetoric to speak of "eternal values" on the basis of their quality, if they are entertained but for a moment. There are no eternal values unless there are eternal valuers.

And the conviction grows that the continuance of life beyond death may be provided for in the universe, without encouraging our imaginations to fall into the old morass.* To the mystic, the certainty of a deathless element in the self is far greater than that of any picture of the mode of continuance. In this respect, the emerging conviction is mystical and reticent.

* Indian religion is not an exception to this rule; though in India it takes the form that the destiny of man is to find union with God, who is the opposite of perishable being. To find this union, classical India has held that the self must be awakened from the illusion of the empirical world: enlightenment is disillusionment and disenthralment. There is in this an excess of rejection, an overdrawn contrast, an unrealisable will to disown time and change themselves. Even so, there is here no exception to the rule that human life reaffirms the value of living, and places the destiny of this life beyond the contingencies of time. And from its excess of rejection of the temporal, Hinduism now draws back.

And in my judgment, this development of the contemporary sense approximates the deeper feeling of unsophisticated mankind. For I believe (in spite of the majestic assemblages of anthropological data rich with the geography of the other world, its furnishings, its social orders, its resolves and purposes, even its events and chronicles) that the faith of the simple has been generally disposed to take its imagery regarding the beyond as poetry rather than literal description. More than we think, popular acquiescence in funereal pomp, extravagance, the purchase of masses, is motivated less by acceptance of priestly theory than by the social significance of observance, the satisfaction of the emotion of the occasion, dislike of the alternative of non-observance, and a dash of the gambler's spirit which desires not to run even a small chance of making an irreparable blunder in supernatural etiquette.

The human self is ready to contemplate its own disappearance if only meaning does not vanish from the universe. Naturalism attempted to meet this requirement that meaning must somehow be conserved by assuring us that the human race will be satisfied whether or not any individual is satisfied. But can meaning be kept if the finite vessels of meaning die? Can the meaning of the whole be conserved if the gains of that abstract essence called "value" are relayed to the latest generations? The evolutionary philosophy has set up a strange picture of racial arrival at illumination and human good, an arrival at the end of time from which all earlier comers are excluded except by anticipation. The vicarious satisfaction which these earlier ones are supposed to take in the prospect is genuine enough. But the whole picture loses verisimilitude when we consider that the illumination of the later ones cannot constitute an answer to the questions of the earlier, and that the satisfaction of the later comers must be desperately qualified by a knowledge that they inherit the efforts of those who can never know to what those efforts have led. If evolutionism is not inherently tragic, it suffers from a radical heartlessness and disloyalty. The soul that contemplates eternity and works for eternity must somehow participate in permanence—this conviction also belongs to the emerging world faith.

THE RECOVERY OF SUPERNATURE

In these several ways, the meanings formerly associated with the term "supernature" are being recovered for sober use, and as it were naturalised.

Until recently a scientific mentality would have been inclined to put the "supernatural" and the "superstitious" in the same brace. But the word "supernatural" has an intelligible etymology, and at once acquires a use when we begin to think of "nature" as a part of the universe, instead of the whole of it.

This is now a usual mode of thought. For in the course of the radical re-examination of the concepts of physical science, these concepts are commonly "constructed" from the presented totality of "experience." The material which is chosen for this construction of the idea of physical nature must be the measurable stuff which lends itself to mathematical relations.

However much of experience is taken into the system of nature, there is a remainder. For example, the feelings and interests of the self which is doing the constructing are no part of the construction. What is to be done with the *qualities* of the physical things, as distinct from their quantities, and with the *life* of living things in nature, is still an unsolved question. And there is always something beyond physical nature— not contained in the space-time system of measured events—as that upon which nature depends.

In brief, these efforts to make precise our conceptions of nature make it clear that, in so far as nature is an object of science, it is a part of the universe, not the whole of it. There is a larger use of the term "nature" which may be made coextensive with the whole; but taking it as scientific method now inclines to outline it, nature is something which takes place within the total universe. Or to put the same truth conversely, the total universe contains much that is in a strict sense extra-natural.

In his capacity as man, the scientist will at all times be aware of the larger totality from which "physical nature" is carved. He might be inclined to say, not that there is an order of being above the natural, but rather that nature has an order of being below or within the real; it might be more reasonable to speak of the sub-reality of physical nature than of the super-naturalness of what is beyond it.

Nevertheless, he may also at times become aware of this reality beyond nature as of something *felt through* nature. It may touch him with a sense of kinship. He may find himself drawn into a certain sympathy with the "procession of natural forms,"* and through them perceiving a life of which nature is the veil.

In such ways as this, whether we speak of a recovery of supernature, or simply of the shift which has taken place in the position of "nature," the change has gone far to create a permissive sanction for such emergent elements of a world faith as we have so far touched upon.

NEMESIS OF HUMANISM

THIS new approach to the supernatural amounts to a solution of the problem set by "humanism," at once a victory for and a liquidation of this movement.

Humanism as I here mean it is the revolt against the old supernature, including the ineffable One of the mystics and the inaccessible Absolute of the philosophers. It was a revolt in the name of a religion which should mean something to human life. It pushed all the objections to the supernatural which were felt by the secular common sense of mankind; but it differed from secularism by retaining religion—it

* "A feeling of oneness with the unending procession of living forms that has marched and marches with unresting feet through time, stepping from death to death, but itself not dying. . . . And there is the primitive, elemental sense of community with the friendly, all-sustaining earth. . . . Men may be much out of doors and remain strangers to nature's ways and moods; but opening a hospitable imagination to the revolving year, they come under the influence of a redemptive intimacy . . . the human spirit is lifted above pettiness and distraction and rendered immune to the fevered insanity frequently identified with civilisation."—Professor M. C. Otto, speaking in the guise of the atheist, in *Is there a God?*, pp. 309, 310.

made a religion of man for man. It was not lacking in
an object for loyalty and devotion, perhaps for worship:
there are powers in the world which make for righteousness—finite, temporal, verifiable powers; there is
always the group spirit, so far as that spirit is devoted
to ideal ends. The passion of such a religion merges
easily with the great social passions. This battle of
humanism has been in substance won. But note what
it is that has been won.

The positive point has been won—that all the doctrine of religion must have its human significance.
The negative point—that all doctrine must give up
its superhuman dimension—has been rejected. It
has been rejected not alone as unnecessary to the
positive point, but as inconsistent with it. For nobody
doubts the human significance of human things; it is
the superhuman significance of human things that
has to be maintained, and if there are no superhuman
things, then there is no religion, and no humanism.

The revolt against the useless and detached transcendental aspect of religion has to be fought many
times in human history. It is of the same stripe as the
pragmatic revolt against an aloof and irresponsible
a priori knowledge. But the outcry that the Absolute
is dead, or that the transcendent has been abolished,
is always premature? While this cry is being raised,
the transcendent returns by another door—the supernatural is recovered in direct connection with inner
experience, as we have just seen. If the Absolute alone
will not serve as God—and it will not—neither will
any finite being, nor any function of human society,

taken alone. It requires the co-operation of the finite and the infinite to make a usable god for mankind.

The correction of humanism is this: that it must be God who is thus discerned in the world, not a substitute.

And this is the nemesis of humanism as a programme of world faith.

A "religion of man" in the sense of Tagore's striking appeal must be set up, but cannot be set up by itself. This religion, which is definitely conceived as a revulsion from the emptiness of India's Absolute, is a religion of the divine man, the *guru* or teacher in whom the divine essence is most palpably present. The guru transmits the Vedas, the spiritual sources; he becomes the second parentage. "The first birth is from the parents; the second birth is from the teacher." He remains in a peculiarly intimate relation to his pupil throughout life, as the transmitter of the divine life. It is this function of transmission which Tagore would sublimate into the accessible object of worship; man inlighted with divinity is to replace the separated God. But what is conveyed by the adjective "divine? If there is no God, nothing is godlike! The adjective cannot keep its meaning if the substantive is let go. Further, these "divine men," wherever we find them, had pointed beyond themselves to an ultimate reality: if they were mistaken, they cease to be good guides. To believe in them is to believe in their belief: to denounce their deity is to reduce them to the common level.

How are we to think of this verifiable aspect of God?

The perception of God for us mortals is always by way of something or through something: it is "mediated." Through what sort of thing men have thought they discerned God—in nature or in human life or in ideal objects—we well know. Humanism was for taking the medium or "mediator" as the goal of our devotion: where we admire or love or are moved as by a premonition of the infinite—there worship! That is simply the original polytheism of mankind, with the omission of the reference of these objects beyond themselves to the god. When we see, as the experiment shows, that we cannot omit the reference-beyond, and keep the meaning of the objects, they resume their role as mediators. Love between human beings, for example, is no point blank attraction: it is always by way of third objects, the common End.* Subconsciously or consciously, to love another is to be drawn to a god.

Through such mediation, God becomes for our perception as real as the human world, as real as things, as real as ourselves! This is not the final standard of reality; it is a frail and defective standard. Yet it is a part of the true standard, for a god who could not thus appear by way of the flesh, or who must remain forever apart from all particular, sensible, historical fact would be indeed an incomplete and unverifiable being. This is the element of justice in the contention of humanism.

It is presumably God's intention that man should discover and know him by way of his own experience.

* See above, p. 33.

If this is true, the whole empirical side of man's search for God—finding him through these mediators and learning that it is the same One who there so variously appears, and what manner of One it is—all this search for God is at the same time God's search for man, and his self-revelation.

Whoever has thus discerned God through his objects becomes, whether he will or not, another such object, a vehicle through whom the discernment of God may spread, as was Origen to Gregory.* The God of whom he speaks to men in word and deed is a God who through him has become newly accessible, has begun to take on as it were a human face. This is the universal conception of the Christ: the Christ is the human face of God.

Thus it turns out that humanism has led to a new grasp of a doctrine which is perhaps of all doctrines the most repugnant both to humanism and to the secular sense, the doctrine of incarnation, the "Word become flesh," the god appearing in the guise of man. Just this idea is the outcome of the rightful demand that the Absolute shall be humanised. It is not, to be sure, the specific doctrine with which we are familiar, nor is it the avatar doctrine of the Indian Vaishnavites; it is more general than they. But just on this account it merges naturally with all the poetry and love of the world, and ties the diverse loyalties of men everywhere to a supreme and single loyalty. It is the most remarkable advance which can be ascribed to the spiritual discernments of an age schooled in realism, that this wider view of "incarnation" is also to be reckoned among the emerging elements of insight.

* See above, p. 38.

2

THE ROLE OF CHRISTIANITY

WITH these emerging filaments of faith—a belief in obligation, in a source of things which is good, in some kind of permanence for what is real in selfhood, and in the human aspect of deity—we have once more an incipient "natural religion," perhaps more intimately possessed than any earlier brand, because of its roots in immediate experience. It is at the same time an aggravated instance of religion in general, attaining such universality as it has only by virtue of omitting everything which constitutes "a" religion.

This rudimentary faith confronts and is confronted by every actual living religion. It does not present itself as a rival, because it has no corporate entity and no voice except the voice of the much-venturing interpreter. It does, however, present an unconscious rivalry to all such particular religions in the sense that it leans heavily on its own meagreness; its reticence is the condition under which it exists at all for vast numbers of mankind. It is something; and having achieved this little at great cost, it is likely to hold itself as better in its poverty than anything more concrete and particular.

In view of our earlier discussions, we will not be under any illusion of its sufficiency as a religion for mankind. Yet I believe that in the next stages of approach to a world faith, the role of any religion will be very largely determined by its relation to these *disjecta membra* of a possible world faith. This role will be very little governed by the official definitions; it will indeed be determined partly by what the religion in question is given out to be, but more by what it is generally reputed to be, and chiefly by what mankind can discover in it. It will be governed less by its priests than by its laymen, and less by either than by the need of the wider world, which is the voice of God admonishing the custodians.

It is therefore our most immediate question how Christianity relates itself to these emerging elements.

Christianity is certainly something more than they in their vagueness and absence of personal focus. It is more than they in authority and certainty of speech. It is more than they in having become the vital energy of a spreading historical movement. Further, it is different in its richness of content: men of a hundred types have found nourishment in it and have left gifts in its treasury. It is no meagre minimum of faith, nor does it profess any admiration for meagreness.

Yet if we ask *what it is* that is being thus defined, lived, injected as a yeast into the vat of history, my answer would be that this *what* or substance of Christianity does approximate these elements. It might be rudely described as the embodied and clarified anticipation, by some two thousand years, of these very convictions to which the groping soul of man after much wandering now slowly and vaguely turns.*

* The scope of these lectures has not allowed more than an incidental expounding of the great religions. The brief indications which I can give here

THE NATURE OF CHRISTIANITY

Christianity affirms what the groping of our time surmises, a source of things which is good; but it declares this source a Father whose aggressive love and care for his individual creatures extends to their particular fortunes. It affirms what the conscience of mankind intuits, an obligation very close to the immediate centre of experience; but it defines this obligation as a duty to be like the Father in love to him and to his creatures. It affirms a future life in which the questions of the soul receive answers and judgment becomes self-judgment. It demands that the will of God be incarnated in the deeds of men; it presents a supreme instance of such incarnation.

We cannot forget that the origin of this religion was in a stupendous effort to pass from the external and intricate corpus of a highly developed religious system to its central spirit. The opposition which the Teacher aroused was due not to new notions which he introduced, but to existing ones which he declared unessential, and to the personal authority which he claimed in making his drastic revaluations. It was the essence of Judaism which he sought—"for this *is* the law and the prophets"—but what he found was a core of faith which seekers after God under all names and none could recognise as answering their unspoken meaning.

Even in the trappings we have made for it, something of its native clarity shines through with emancipating

of the nature of Christianity are supplemented by a statement made in another connection and here reprinted as an appendix (p. 277). I hope shortly to return to this theme in a separate volume.

force. Hu Shih regards himself as a naturalist philosopher and a critic of all organised religion, especially of those other-worldly types from which China has had so much to suffer; yet it is Hu Shih who, looking at Christianity as a phenomenon in China, judges that it is relatively free from superstition and demands a relative purity of life; further, that the transitional misfits which it produces are not to be too severely censured, since in any period of new orientation, and weaning from the past, such moods must occur.* Wherever it goes, Christianity tends to serve as a clarifying agency, reducing the complexities and extraneous loads of religion, giving the human mind a property in its world-view, and an insight into the meaning of the will of God, freeing the human will from the burden of opaque acceptance.

But note, too, that this "simple essence" we speak of is not limited to the teaching of the Sermon on the Mount. It is the great gain of the present moment in history that the emerging faith has come, in the way we have traced, upon the human sense of the idea of incarnation. This mystery has become to just this extent generally intelligible—a quality rightly regarded in theological quarters with suspicion, yet not necessarily treasonable! And with this gain the meaning of Christianity has become much more accessible to mankind at large.

* Conversation, 1932. Here I am moved to quote Dean Inge's citation of Bishop Hall, a seventeenth-century divine, who said that "the most useful of all books on theology would be one with the title, De Paucitate Credendorum, or the fewness of the things which a man must believe."— Things New and Old, 1933, p. 48.

Men have always been ready to do homage to the teachings of Jesus, as beautiful statements of an impracticable ideal. They are prepared to incorporate these ideals in their own codes. They have halted at the doctrine of "the divine Word made flesh." They have not seen that without the entrance of deity into human life the Sermon on the Mount can neither be practised nor understood. Hence the radicalism of that Sermon remains to them poetry, an extravagance, fanatical; it refuses to connect with conduct, draws down the just reproach of the Moslem and the Hindu that it is beyond reach, leaves Christendom itself with a divided conscience if not a besetting hypocrisy.

When is it possible to take no thought for the morrow? *When* can one turn the other cheek? *When and how* can one love one's neighbour as oneself? These are not modes of behaviour of which one can say: To-day I will do them. There is no use in taking on these attitudes unfelt: this is the curse of our public professions of benevolence and pacific good-will; for the most part they are grimaces unfilled with conviction and unblessed by spontaneity—they have no *Tao* in them. In view of our actual dispositions we have to regard the Sermon less as a code which we can forthwith go out and practise than as a prayer: "May we be pure in heart; may we love our enemies; may we touch the rim of the perfectness of God . . ." The Sermon is a code for a transformed man. I am called upon to act as if *in loco Dei* to my small world; only as this new dimension of being is born in me from beyond myself can I do this naturally, love my neighbour genuinely, and without futility because the same temper is brought to pass in him. The Sermon presupposes that the incarnation of God's will which took place in Jesus is to take place in us also; apart from this it loses usableness.

And without this, there can be no basis for our much-invoked and more-violated "sacredness" of human personality, not for "equality," nor for the "rights of man," nor for the inner vitality of western civilisation, nor for any enduring human tie. Without the general meaning of incarnation, the ideals of the Sermon become moral tantalizations and deceiving lights, luring ourselves and our societies into a bog of incapacity for determined action, torn by standards which we neither know how to use nor how to surrender.

But there is something incomplete about the general idea of incarnation, as there is about the general idea of a fact! Christianity does not rest in the generality. It refers to the birth of the Idea in the world, its idea of things, as a special deed of God. It puts this deed into the essence of its faith. Incarnation-in-general is one of the bits of idle poetry unless there is incarnation in particular.

Christianity has no need to deny that the will of God appears and has appeared in many deeds in many lands. Its concern is affirmative; but for the confirming of its case it has to light upon an unquestionable instance, and it requires but one. Hence it was bound to present its case thus: "Here, at least, God is visible, and in a way clear to all men; here at least there is victory over suffering and death; here at least we see the human being exercising a divine forgiveness. Here at least the general symbol of the mediator, the Christ, becomes a literal particular."

The instinct of mankind, when confronted by a generality of religion or philosophy, is to say "Show me by an illustration what you mean" or "Show me by an accomplished fact that your way is possible." The demand is peculiarly justified if the generality in question is this, that the divine may take human shape. The moral tetanus due to the rooted suspicion of human nature (which is our most radical sin) that the ideal is a *mere ideal*, an eternal Platonism, has to be broken. To break that palsy would be to release for action the torrent of the pent-up idealism of mankind, and this would be the saving of the world.

If anything could do this deed of breaking and release, it would be a demonstration—Behold, here, one ideal made fact. Christianity therefore cannot dispense with its illustration; it must set it into its creed. Such an item readily becomes, in the hands of two extremes, the timorous and the tyrannical, the bludgeon of the Only Way. But its original significance was purely positive, and as we now see, necessary.

The perfection of an illustration lies chiefly in two things, its sufficiency and its just-sufficiency. The Christian illustration has these attributes of perfection; it is adequate, and it carries no superfluous load. We know so little of the factual life of Jesus that it is possible to imagine (and for some scholars to believe) the narratives a myth: a fortunate ignorance has severely limited to the significant the details of the picture. Yet the veridical traits of actuality are there;

and the full Idea is embodied. Christianity is the only religion which inclines to substitute its founder for its entire doctrine, and knows that it has gained rather than lost by so doing.

This disposition to fund its meaning in the person of Jesus Christ has the merits of summary concreteness, of escape from the strait-jackets of creedal definitions, and of conveying the truth that truth is personal. Further, it is able to anticipate all future growth; for the now immaterial figure is no longer a receding shade but the infinite forerunner: at whatever point we arrive in our search for truth, the risen Christ, freed from limit and from time-limit by death, is conceived to have been there before us. This same disposition has equally many dangers: the danger of condoning mental laziness in a fogginess of content which may claim everything and evade everything*; the danger of softness of commitment, a slippery and purring readiness to "follow Jesus," with a preference for vagueness as to what "Jesus" stands for; the danger of assuming that Jesus himself was unable to say what he meant in terms of concepts—a defeatism of the divine intelligence! And with all this there is the commonly accepted invitation to make a shibboleth of the name, declining into a word-and-figure worship increasingly repellent to the contemporary sense for reality in religion.

In spite of these abuses, the greatest strength of Christianity is its symbol, with its unimaginable

* On this account, it lends itself admirably to the exigencies of ecclesiastical diplomacy: to say, for example: "Our message is Jesus Christ" will always fetch a majority, for the phrase conjoins indubitable soundness with an almost perfect economy of thought.

depth, beauty, and power. This life and its record are a treasure so far transcending lines of time and place, race and sect, that even with the antipathies aroused by partisan advocacy, it slowly makes its way as a possession of mankind.

To summarise: In stating the essence of religion, Christianity has had a certain time-advantage, because it started with that end in view. The general movement of world-thinking, secular and otherwise, now tends to meet it half-way. Some of its doctrines have taken on human verifiability.* And while men still distrust the

* If we approach the doctrinal content of Christianity in this way, by proceeding from the whole to the part, we find that many of its special doctrinal forms become luminous, and present wide possibilities of helping our speculative groping.

For example, there are still extant tangles regarding monotheism, poly-theism, pantheism—less remote from the verifiable human interest than their names convey—toward whose solution the doctrine of the Trinity has important suggestions to make.

The stricter monists (Jews and Moslems) consider that they have still to wage the fight against idolatry in the other religions and also against that compromise of God with the disorder and evil of the world found in all immanence-theologies and in idealism. The Trinity is interpreted by them as a limited polytheism: the Koranic refrain to the effect that Allah neither begets nor is begotten is directed against it. Nevertheless, these religions also have their own mediators and their mystics; their own origins are referred to some kind of conversation between God and man; they also cannot do without the human aspect of God.

And while the doctrine of the Trinity remains a mystery over which subtleties may be endlessly poured out as intellectual libations, in its total tangible effect it is an admonition that pure monotheism is not enough, whereas tri-theism is too much and too many; the true idea of God lies between them; it must at least contain a procession out of the infinite reserve into the life of the universe and of men, and without abandoning its absolute self-hood. This doctrine is probably much more valuable as a mystery to be jealously guarded from solution than in any possible philosophical transla-tion. For as a mystery, it stands simply for the indispensable parameters of any tenable idea of God.

bonds of the specific channels which Christianity must propose, they begin to see also that there can be no living religion without some specific channel; and that while any particular taken by itself is arbitrary and irrational, any other particular would be equally so. The virtue of the particular Fact is not that it is necessary—no Fact can ever be that—but that it may become indispensable, as the fit, historical, unrepeatable Symbol of a truth which *is* necessary.

CHRISTIANITY AND WESTERN CIVILISATION

THE availability of Christianity—its advantage, if we may adopt for a moment the external language of rivalry—is not wholly of that intrinsic nature to which we have been addressing ourselves. There are non-religious advantages, apparently accidental, wholly apart from its merits, due to its entanglement with western civilisation.

Thus, it is a notable asset of Christianity that it has a superior *power of self-expression*. It is not merely a matter of the obstacles of language that the explanations offered by a Buddhist priest or a Hindu pundit will fall into a somewhat strict pattern from which he does not easily depart. Christianity has wider resources of self-definition and of apology. It has lived for two millennia in company with a diverse activity in western philosophising and in letters, and for three hundred years with a group of independent sciences. Alone among the great religions, Christianity has fought out its issues with the natural sciences, has passed through the purge of the scientific study of itself as an object, its "higher criticism," its comparative science of religion, its psychology of religion. It has met outspoken criticism on the part of these free agencies; and it has gained from this ordeal a capacity not alone to defend itself but to perceive what is defensible and what not defensible. It no longer feels the necessity of denouncing scientific results in the interest of a literal biblical loyalty. It has ceased for the most part, to identify itself with scientific absurdities; it has been disciplined, hardened, and made agile. By reducing its appanage of cumulative fancy, science has given Christianity the fighting benefit of its inherent simplicity, and a language soberly responsible to experience.

It is hardly accurate to call this advantage accidental, since (contrary to the common reading of history) Christianity is largely responsible for this very independence which makes the arts and sciences such telling critics. It is Christianity which has set the arts free, and defined the grounds of their secular operation. For example, John of Damascus stated the separation of philosophy from theology; Augustine used and expanded the distinction; Thomas Aquinas gave it a systematic place; on this basis Descartes could give philosophy a wholly secular head, and propose for it a method derived from mathematics and physics. Since Galileo, Christian theology has had the criticism not alone of science and philosophy but also of a social order increasingly disposed to conduct its affairs on an experimental basis. All religions have had an attendant corps of scholars; but it is one thing to discuss with a group of minds submissive to an ultimate authority; another to debate with minds who have thought out and apply their own criteria of truth and reality.

Again, alone among the great religions, Christianity is accustomed to a *free social application*. Many another of the living religions is embedded in a set of social customs: to all local religions it is an axiom that religion belongs with law and the institutions. But just because local religions exist as already applied, it is difficult to apply them! A principle can be applied, a regulation cannot be. A principle can be applied to a particular situation, new or old, because it is *not yet committed* to a fixed rule. It permits the question of application because it exists as the spirit of the laws, not as a code of law. Christianity enjoys this freedom of principle. From the first it has held itself clear of social doctrines; it is not a social gospel; the precepts of the Sermon, taken literally, promote detachment from institutions and from the arts. Yet Christianity is socially responsible; it established premises from which social conclusions can be drawn and are constantly being drawn. It defines an attitude towards the neighbour and his goods from which legislation may always enquire its direction. Christianity is used to being applied.

If Confucianism or Islam is to be applied to present conditions, it has first to gain detachment from its specific codes. The Shiekh of Al Azhar takes the decisive step when he proposes that the legislation of Egypt be based on the spirit of the Koran, not on the letter—theft, for example, is not punished in Egypt as Wahabi orthodoxy requires and has in Ibn Sa'ud's country very recently practised, by cutting off the hand. The next step is to determine what in terms of principle the Koranic spirit is: upon that step it will not be too easy to reach agreement. Buddhism has the requisite separateness of principle, but not the habit of being socially applied—it lacks the tradition of concern for the social order. It is undertaking to develop such a tradition; and especially in Japan is making progress in philanthropic and educational enterprise. But it has to build the habit of mind, and the personnel for this work.* Christianity stands ready to hand; its members have not alone the habit of free and new social thinking, but also the incentive and the ideal.

In both of these ways, interaction with western civilisation has made Christianity relatively mature; it is prepared to give the aid of maturity to cultures whose sciences have been less caustic, and whose social changes less inclined to claim the sanction of free ethical principle.

It is a further advantage that Christianity has developed its own *common people*, and is in this respect democratic.

It has never admitted for long the aristocratic trait

* A Buddhist business man of Osaka said to me in 1932, "Buddhism is our religion, but its social thought is not vigorous nor swift enough for this great period of transition in Japan. We must rely on Christianity for help. We must have time and must gain in experience; we are beginning. You must help us."

of the Orient, the acceptance of mental distance, with priestly authority and esoteric enlightenment on one side and a mixture of esoteric doctrine and popular superstition on the other. The common people have been the first objects of its care; its preaching has been to them rather than to other specialists—as Buddha spoke first to the monks; it is "the poor" who have to be rescued from their blind guides. It is true that the dullness of the crowd led the Teacher of the narratives to turn with special instruction to those "who had ears to hear"; but the barrier is there to be broken down, and as often as an esoteric understanding has appeared in the history of the Church, it has been dissolved. The public eventually has its "Great Bible." And since their own spiritual understandings have been not only permitted but called for, the mental activity of the laity has kept the priestly orders alive and spurred to thought. This requirement has carried with it all the troubles incident to democratic assumptions—the flattery of the common conceit that it, too, may be authoritative and dictate to its betters. But the burden of persuasion thus thrown on the betters has been much to the benefit of their powers to think and to teach. And the masses have been mentally prepared to give body to any movement requiring new thinking. Religion becomes a common life, with a common fund of feeling, ready for common tasks.

But with these advantages goes the most serious disadvantage: in its embroilment with western civilisation and history, Christianity has become not alone in the opinion of the Orient but in fact a *western religion*.

Had it been less fertile, less frequently applied to social issues, it might have retained more of its original aloofness and unprovincial quality. Buddhism is freer in this respect: in its literary sources and doctrines, it still speaks to man; Vedanta is almost purely non-local. But Christianity has had to perform the functions of the local religion for the West; and in so doing it has taken on something more than a veneer of western manners, forms of expression in music, architecture and the rest. There adhere to it beliefs in our form of the family as a necessary form, in our modes of property as somehow bound up in Christianity, in our forms of law and government—diverse as they are—as sanctioned by our God; so also our customs, our prejudices, and at times our interests. This involvement with western culture, which was once an asset when intellectual Asia was avid for the secrets of western power and supposed that religion had them, has now become a detriment of unknown proportions. Acceptance of such a thoroughly concreted Christianity amounts, in the new Orient, to adopting a party attitude, the party of the foreigner and perhaps of the foreign master.

That Christianity in the East attempts to divest itself of these local accretions we have seen: its presence in Asia forces upon it a self-consciousness of localism which aids this separation. There is no need here to dwell on less creditable circumstances in which the Church has accepted, and given, political aid; nor to assess the degree to which it is still true that missions from certain southern European states vibrate sympathetically with the interests of those powers. In the great majority of cases, Christianity in Asia is disinterested, fears its own localism, and makes valiant attempts to distinguish its essence from its assumed burdens. But this work, however sincere, is a matter of extreme difficulty: not even our wide awareness of relativity in morals and manners cures the ingrained conviction that most of what we believe and do is inherently necessary and universal.*

The effort is the more difficult because much of western civilization *does in fact go with Christianity*; and the religion cannot wholly repudiate its own children, even when those children repudiate their maternal ancestry! The situation is not simple; and it is of the first importance to become clear as to what it is. Christianity is said to be western; and yet frequently the same critics will assert that western civilisation is not Christian. In my own judgment, the case is just the reverse: Christianity is not incurably western; and yet, since it has begotten certain features of the West, western civilisation is to that extent incurably Christian! Let me explain.

Western civilisation is certainly not Christian in its deeds. All of its agencies in politics, commerce, and the arts have declared their secular independence, and this relation is accepted by the Church. The religion is relieved of direct responsibility for whatever is done, except when it expressly sanctions what is done:†

* In a Christian girls' school in Japan, a request was made at Christmas time by some of the students that they might be allowed to decorate the room in the way familiar to them, setting bunches of fir boughs in the corners. The headmistress declined: "Only the Christmas tree is pleasing to God," she said.

† It is perhaps necessary to our discussion to mention that of recent international crimes, two of the three most conspicuous and brutal have been carried out with the equally public blessing of the Church. This fact has not been lost on Asia.

Christianity cannot in general be held for the crimes of western politics; it cannot be held for the outbreak of war! To those in the Orient—and they are many—who count the war of 1914 as a failure of Christianity, it has to be said that Christianity was not applied to the situation; and since it was not tried, it was not a failure! It failed in the deeper sense that it lacked influence on the event: it had already failed to convince the governments of Europe that it was worth trying; I presume it failed to propose anything concrete which the governments could try. There was not in the world then, nor is there now, any Christian foreign policy.

Now the Church—as it learns its normal relation to the State—is unwilling to seek a remedy for this situation by regaining control of the deeds of governments or of business. Men and governments must be free to go wrong. The Church remains free to advise if it has advice to offer; and through its members it is free to criticise the State or to influence by their votes the policy of the State; but it rejects the position in which it could compel any State to accept its advice. To this extent Christianity may wash its hands of direct responsibility for western behaviour, though it can take but a funereal satisfaction in doing so.

But if not in its deeds, in its structure western society is Christian. Western science and western law have had Christianity as one of their parents. Not that the religion has written any law, or produced any scientific truth; but that the codes and empirical attitude are, on one side, of Christian parentage. The situation is paradoxical. The arts are free from religion; this freedom is itself a part of western structure which

Christianity has promoted; yet the nature of the freedom is such as to leave no art self-sufficient. None of them can retain its vitality in complete severance from the religious background. This is the point so easily overlooked both by western historians and sociologists, and by oriental observers. For example, the civil codes of Europe are based on some assumption of natural human rights and on some convention of human equality: they seldom make explicit reference to religion and in the era of the French Revolution expressly repudiated any such connection. But it is clear that on the basis of pure naturalism, men are not equal, and the term "rights" has no meaning. On this account, if a western community could be completely secularised, it would fail to work; a secularised democracy does fail to work—it flatters men without providing the salt of either humility or love of neighbour. In proportion as secularisation becomes complete, the characteristic codes of Europe and the parliamentary constitutions cease to function, and the State tends to revert to the totalitarian form, which is not distinctively western nor distinctively Christian. In sum, all characteristic western institutions assume for their success a type of *morale* whose vitamin has to be generated by the religious background: with every freedom from institutional attachment, there remains an actual dependence.

For this reason, the belief that aspects of western civilisation can be borrowed without borrowing the religion which begot them is illusory. It is the common belief in the newer Oriental states. Our science can be taken, our modes of commerce, our codes, our technology; and as for our religion, that can be left behind. A Japanese Commission sent to America some years ago reported that Christianity counted for nothing in public life, and could be ignored. The question has been raised in Turkey whether the adoption of so many European practices and ideas would or should bring with it an adoption of the European religion, and with a similar conclusion: the western codes can be used, but on the basis of the sociology of Emil Durkheim. A Moslem writing recently from Beirut sees somewhat farther: a "Christian ethics," he argues, is the only answer to the present chaos in the world; he sees the pagan elements in so-called Christian civilisation, but considering that no religion has all its own way, he observes that where Christianity has really come there has been progress. He urges that this ethics be developed within the frame of Islam:

> We are continuously borrowing from you. We borrow your thoughts, your method, your outlook, but due to this non-intercourse position you have taken, we have been forced to keep our attitude of enmity towards you. What we have borrowed is transplanted into a hostile atmosphere . . . dwarfed and biased, it cannot bear abundant fruits. . . . We do not want to remain a drag on world progress. We want to join you in world reconstruction. But we want at the same time to retain our identity. You have to take it out of your mind that Islam is a passing fad. It has come here to stay. Rather than destroy Islam you ought to fill in its gaps.*

The experience of the farther East runs towards a

* From the *Moslem World*, July 1937, p. 295-7.

perception that the secularised fragments of civilisation do not stand by themselves—they require an ethic. And after defining the ethic, we still require to fill the sails of that ethic, in some way, with the spirit of the faith it came from.

However, then, Christianity may be clogged, barnacled and misrepresented by its western entanglements, and however we must insist on its free and separate character, there is something in that westernism that goes and ought to go with Christianity, namely those parts which, like a free science, have already shown their universality, and which are making their own way in the world without propaganda. To this extent, Christianity is and should be western; and westernism is and should be Christian, even though it feels itself emancipated.

It is, I believe, the chief of these "accidental" advantages of Christianity that it has worked its way to the solution of this paradox of independence and dependence: it has found the true dialectical balance between its universal and its local elements. It has the grit in it which requires it to affect the locality, and to become itself localised; yet it remains free from bondage to *this* locality, and can assume similar free relations to others. It has learned through experience that only in a "secular" civilisation (autonomous in its arts) can religion itself become mature. At the same time it asserts (and civilisation discovers through *its* experience) that only in presence of a free religion can a community life be both fertile and stable.

Through these very circumstances of its entanglement, Christianity may indicate the key whereby the resources of all civilisations may be unlocked. But the nature of its association with western history requires to be clarified, both to itself and to the rest of the world. It must be clear what its relationship is and can be to the new nations of the east; that it can favour an honest nationalism anywhere, and an aggressive nationalism nowhere; that it must submit to whatever discredit is involved in having an international character, an international ethic, and a super-national responsibility. Of all the intellectual aids to the spread of Christianity, the most important would be a realistic philosophy of its own history in its relation to civilisation.

CHRISTIANITY IS NOT YET READY TO SERVE AS A WORLD RELIGION

LIKE every living being, Christianity has two selves— its potential, or ideal self, and its empirical or actual self. The latter is the Christianity of our present grasp and practice. In its ideal character, Christianity is the "anticipation of the essence" of all religion, and so contains potentially all that any religion has. But it is quite too complacent to say this of the Christianity of our apprehension: if that were true there would be no need of further efforts to grasp the essence. When, therefore, a Christian scholar writes that the change from harsh and ignorant criticism of other religions to warm appreciation "need not lead us to forget that Christ still offers to men of every creed and race all that they have hitherto treasured, and beyond that yet other gifts far surpassing their power to imagine"* he is referring to the ideal Christianity, which is also far beyond our own reach: it hardly conduces to just estimates to give ourselves the credit for our unrealized assets while taking other faiths at their present face value.

There are two things which remind us constantly that our grasp is faulty. First, that we have not solved our own problems of the bearing of Christianity on any social institution, more particularly on war, property, the family. Second, that there are still values outside of Christianity, in other religions, which we think ought not to perish.

As to the social problems of our time, Christianity is indeed accustomed to being applied, and to being sought out for guidance. But in our present quandaries, it must be confessed that it seems less rather than more prepared to furnish such guidance. Separated by its own principle from a controlling hand in the secular life of man, it loses intuitive perception of the meaning of the changing issues. It is prepared to water the roots of political and commercial sagacity by its admonitions to good will and peace; but these qualities fail of effect without concreteness of aim and resolution in action. We have said that there is no Christian foreign policy; there is likewise no Christian domestic policy. In my judgment, the occasions are rare when there could be a univocal Christian policy in either

* James Thayer Addison in International Review of Missions; reviewed in *World Christianity*, Autumn, 1938, pp. 42–46.

sphere; there should, however, be a plenum rather than a dearth of competent thought, and with an active trend toward consensus. There should be at least an available ethical judgment of the ethical aspect of public policies. But what is the present status of Christian judgment in respect to war, to economic justice, to nationalism on their ethical sides?

As to war and pugnacity, we see the problems treated as if the answer could be read from the surface of Scripture: "Christianity does away with both: it teaches love of enemy, meekness, non-resistance." And is that all? Then were Marx and Bakunin right when they said of it, as of all religion, that it makes its adherents as sheep before the shearers? Is there nothing in Christianity to spur men to oppose injustice (to others as well as to themselves) or to fight for a decenter world?* Then Christianity has lost its original dimension of moral greatness. For we cannot forget that Christianity has been the one religion under which men have fought for rights, their own and others' and under which, because of this, civil law in Europe has grown strong. It has had a structural force not found elsewhere. Its "love" has not lacked the salt of just pugnacity. It has contained in solution all that

* A student of marked ability, a negro, was hesitating between going into the ministry and entering the American Association for the Advancement of Coloured People. In the one, he said, he would have to remind his people constantly of the duties of love, forgiveness, long-suffering; in the other he would have to admonish them to resent wrong and to stand up for their rights; and as he put it, "My people need both of these things." True enough; but must they have one-half of what they need from Christianity and the other half from a secular source? Then the religion does indeed serve as an opiate and a half-truth!

sternness which Nietzsche demanded, even though a Nietzsche was required to remind it of what in solution it had. When now Dr. Ambedkar of India says that Christians have lost their capacity for moral indignation, he sends an unhappily telling shaft. The supposition that the teaching of Jesus may have meant supine acquiescence before well-armed iniquity, or the emitting of friendly bleatings thoroughly unmeant, stands as a reproach less to the virility of the faith than to the virility of contemporary interpretation.

Nor is Christianity more ready to guide our judgments about property and social justice. It is discontent with a non-partisan aloofness. It is equally discontent with a partisan position; for how can it exclude from its membership either one or the other of the opposing views, either (let us say) capitalist or communist, either individualist or corporativist?

But if the Church cannot be a party, must it therefore be a nonentity in these matters? Have we not passed through and beyond the era of the Manchester superstition of economic autonomy? Have we not discovered that there are no economic solutions on solely economic grounds? The Christian Church needs the courage to believe in its pertinence to every social situation, and its partisanship in none. It has still to define and exercise the function prescribed by its own genius, that of bringing to the questions which it has no competence to settle, the moral postulates without which there can be no settlement.

Meanwhile contemporary Christianity plainly envies

social and national movements their alleged "religious-ness," their social and patriotic fervour, their capacity for bringing men to the point of single-mindedness and self-sacrifice. This envy is confession that it has lost grip upon its own source of feeling. It has no comparable passion of its own to lift man up and away from the furore of his finite causes. This is because it is rent by the unsatisfied and unsatisfiable demand for a "social gospel"; it is deflected by humanism; it has become semi-ashamed of its other-worldliness, without which it can have no distinctive contribution to any social problem.

Christianity is based on the affirmation that human life gets its meaning and dignity from what is beyond humanity. Without this superhuman reference, it becomes just another social agency, with no especial qualification to be such. With it, it can be no social party—for it has a higher calling; but it can produce the men who can take sides, and reach conclusions, and also the spirit and demand in terms of which conclusions must be reached.

Finally, as Christianity is the best organised of all religions, and in its Catholic forms most adequate to the idea of the Church, so it is most of all in danger of the corruptions attending organisation.

It may be said that Christianity is the only religion in which the demand to "Enter"—i.e. to participate in a definite historic effort (the Kingdom)—was addressed to all members (and not merely to the brotherhood of monks, as in Buddhism). This places a peculiar weight on its structure. But a corresponding effort has to be made to keep that structure sound.

If it cannot clean the stables of priestly greeds, political venalities in high places, connivance in the ambitions of States, and the silent, suave corporate purchasing of mentality and conscience by posts and preferments, it not only surrenders much of its ascendency over the human spirit, but ripens for such days of wrath as overtook the Church of Russia or the vast and beautiful establishments of northern Europe.

In speaking thus of the unreadiness of Christianity, I am but saying what the Christian conscience is now widely aware of. We are, I believe, at the opening of an era of new greatness in the history of Christian thought because we are engaged in a profounder and humbler self-scrutiny than the modern Church has yet known. For the moment, unreadiness is what we are bound to confess, even while we attempt to transmit that ideal Christianity which stands beyond our unreadiness.

OUR PRESENT CHRISTIANITY DOES NOT INCLUDE ALL THAT OTHER RELIGIONS HAVE

WHAT the values in the other religions are, which Christianity does not have, is a matter whose precise determination may never be finished. Perhaps it is not capable of a wholly objective answer. I can certainly not pretend here to give such an answer. But I may give a report of my personal judgments, as I have found here and there in the world expressions of the spirit of the non-Christian religions at their best.

Islam.—Within Islam one is aware of a dignity, a sweep, a sense of the instant majesty of God, which we lack. Among Islamic peoples one sees how the habitual thought about God becomes a part of the personal quality of the man; dignity enters into him also. None of these concepts are lacking to us; nor have they failed to find their way into architecture and music. But they lack saliency in our religious expression and in our lives.

To the Moslem, God in His majesty is also a near and present God. Our mediators aid, and also impede; when we make them objects of worship, they carry a descent. The Moslem never forgets that it is God with whom he has to do. If his escape from the intermediate clutter leaves him stark, it also clarifies his soul.

Islam has also an effective fraternity which crosses racial bounds with an ease which Christianity professes but Christians seldom attain. The solidarity and unimpressionableness of Islam are largely due to the fact that Islam has no proletariat. The book is open to all on the same terms—at least in Arabic; it is the school book of the whole Moslem world. Beneath the sects, the simplicity of the central confession, and the felt pettiness of human distinctions in the sight of Allah, weld its people into a religious unity not realised elsewhere.

Hinduism and Buddhism.—We have already spoken

of the *reflectiveness* of these religions,* their power to state religious truth in its own conceptual medium, rather than to confine it to the narrative-historical mode of statement.

In general, these religions are weak in respect to history, and require the supplement of the Semitic genius. But the need is mutual.

The relief from literalness of the conceptual treatment of religion, in these Indian traditions, is towards mysticism and poetry rather than toward history. The advantage is that poetry and myth are seldom in danger of being confused with reason. In the Semitic religions, the line between narrative and myth is not clear; and the consequence is that western Christianity has never been sure which is its poetry and which its prose. Our persistent loyalties to myth in the guise of history give western Christianity a distinctly stupid and childish air, as compared with the inlighted deftness of touch of the true oriental, especially the Indian mind.

I would mention, too, the naturalness of the meditative element of religion, so that school children know instinctively what is to be done in an hour of "meditation." The psychological principle is accepted that a price must be paid for insight: it is not to be had in the intervals of a packed school-programme; efficiency is a misapprehension of the meaning of the need to realise a thought: time, preparation, and effort must be spent in order to see.

And while, as has been well pointed out, the spirituality of the East dare not ignore the genuine spirituality

* Above, p. 94.

involved in the intrepid drive for truth characteristic of western science, the fundamental ethical discipline of the empirical attitude, it remains true that there is another facet of spirituality still pre-eminently oriental —the willingness among all groups, and not alone among the devotees, to pay the price of spiritual gifts, the capacity to renounce the lesser for the greater.

Christianity is right in locating its life in both worlds, and in refusing to count illusory or evil the apparent reals and goods of the surface of experience; they, too, are the garment of God—or better, the moment-by-moment doings of God. But in its joy at this discovery, it is easily seduced by its own comfort. It too easily takes "prosperity" as a sign of the favour of God, and the harvest festival of thanksgiving as the highest moment of its prayer, the prayer over a heavy meal. The Orient is less a despiser of this world than repute has accused it of being, but it more instantly realises the insidious hold of physical enjoyment on the proportions of moral sanity; and more promptly renounces, with large and magnanimous thoroughness, what it discovers to be a personal peril to the soul.

There remains a third point of excellence: the actually achieved serenity of spirit in many an oriental saint.

It is no idle boast when one of these men gives an affirmative answer to the question, Have you found peace? The old Stoic ideal of the imperturbable man is more frequently realized in India, I surmise, than in any other part of the world to-day, because with the actuality of renunciation there follows at once a freedom from petty fears, from angers, and from anxiety about many things. Compared with the discreditable and unchristian agitation of Christian leaders here and there over the menace of communism or the general state of the world, and the shameful hurry-up campaigns for world-conquest by Christianity, these quietly-great souls may well be a means of ushering Christianity into a region of its own proper meaning.

Buddhism.—In Buddhism I would especially mention a matter which is likely to stir emotions of apprehension in a Christian mind. I mean the enjoyment of the *impersonal element* of ultimate truth.

In my own belief, personality is the deeper and more inclusive category. For a person is capable of entertaining the impersonal, whereas the impersonal has no capacity of itself for entertaining the personal. A person may, for example, school himself to be more like a law of nature, and less subject to whimsical variations of mood; whereas a law of nature has no capacity for developing the quality of personality!

But impersonality belongs, as it were, to the vast inner spaces of God's being. The inability to trust oneself to the enjoyment of the impersonal regularities of the world whether of science or of the moral law— as if regularity, which gives hold to science, must therefore be hostile to religion (as giving a proof of self-operation!), betrays a lack of faith in God and a certain pettiness of religious conception from which the better minds of the Orient are quite free.

Buddhism, in its origins, no doubt tended to err in the other direction, and too fully swept away the personal element which might still be clinging to the notion of the absolute substance, in the interest of absolute law of process; and has, in the dialectic of its own long history been led to compensate for that fault in the growing predominance of the Bodhisattva conceptions, and especially of Amida Buddha, the gracious. But one must still keep open the question whether the corrections have improved the case; in so far as personal deities introduce an opportunist element into the relations of God and man, religion is cheapened rather than enlarged.

It is more easy for Indian than for Christian piety to recognise that the pursuit of truth is a part of the love of God (in Gandhi's view, tending to identity). The Platonic Ideas of Beauty and Goodness are not at once, by the Christian mind, perceived to have anything to do with religion, still less to be ingredients of the nature of God; and loyalty to abstract causes, such as justice or liberty in some specific shape, is likely to take on a purely secular ring. This is partly due to the long struggle of early Christianity with the menace of a Platonism which would have eaten the heart out of its historical concreteness; the battle was rightly decided against the Platonists. But Christianity still suffers from the iniquity of making this a party issue; it remains semi-blind to the majesty of the impersonal element in the being of God, and hence misjudges its own scope.

Confucianism.—It is a very opposite excellence that we find here, namely, its intense humanity. The "filial piety" from which Confucius undertook to deduce the whole duty of man, is based on the assumption that the family tie is at the same time a sacred tie; the family, as an over-personal entity, receiving the spirits of its own dead and continuing their connection with the living, being for its members the nearest medium of access to the heavenly sphere, and the most constantly invoked. That this relationship has been an impediment to progress, as it has been interpreted, no one sees more clearly than the Confucianist of to-day. But that it need be a bar to progress he is ready to deny; and that the new China has need of it he rightly insists. The family organisation changes, the large family dissolves, the exclusive loyalty to all things in the universe via the family is widening into other recognitions, national and abstract. But the obligation of the family to its members, for their education in the moral elements of life, and of its members to it on account of that transmissive function, is as vital to the new China as to the old, and as vital to the new Occident as to the Orient.

The family, like the state, must prepare for its own supercession. It must produce the free individual, and in him risk the loss of its own fabric; for it is only the free individual that can preserve that fabric. China has to learn with pain the secret of the inner strength of the non-communistic schemes of personal life. But the vast inner moral resources of China under present strains may show that her traditional system of "sacred relationships" had been so interpreted as to leave much initiative and self-judgment available as a national resource. The human bonds are destined to give strength to the individual, not to submerge him. And it is this which we in our western skittishness, and rooted distrust of group presumptions, have still to appreciate. If the human bond is veritably a way to God, whether through the modestly estimated virtues of the ancestors—about which the Chinese were little given to effusiveness—or through revulsions against their vices, it is cured, or has in itself the potential cure, of its tyranny.

If the human bond to parents sets itself up as an Absolute it may be reminded, as President Lim would remind it, that parents and ancestors are to be revered *only so far as they are worthy of reverence!* It is the function of the valid Absolute to keep all relatives reminded of their relativity. With this in mind the Chinese conception of the human bonds as mediator of the divine becomes significant for all religion, not excluding Christianity.

I would also mention the prevalent cheerfulness and naturalness of the Confucian conception of religion; one might speak of its inner gaiety.

This is sometimes ascribed to a Chinese deficiency in the sense of sin, the peculiar grace which gives to Christianity its deep disturbing, chastening and therefore rebuilding power. And I quite agree that contrition is a sign of depth, provided it comes without being worked for. The question is, however, not whether any person or race is sufficiently depressed in view of its defectiveness, but whether it is capable of perceiving the ideal at all; for if it perceives the ideal and is self-conscious, the judgment of its distance from perfection is not escapable, nor the question of what it can do to be cured. In itself, the perception of the ideal is a joy; and the normal attitude of the Christian is not one of despair, but one of gratitude that he has recognised the standard which at once condemns him and exalts him. In this normal attitude, it is not unlikely that China, which is not deficient in its sense of the standard, may still have something to teach us. For gaiety also is not without its route to holiness, as Gilbert Chesterton saw when he wrote his phrase, "the giant laughter of Christian men."*

I do not suggest that these impressions of mine touch even the most important of the idiosyncrasies of non-Christian faiths. I mention them somewhat at random as characteristics which may typify the problem which Christianity as a world-faith would have to meet. No religion could present itself as the completion of other faiths until it had gone through the labour of understanding those faiths. And this labour no religion has as yet more than begun. The proposition that "Jesus Christ includes everything," however valuable as a postulate of faith to be made good by the thoughtful effort of the believer, when set up as an *a priori* basis for the intercourse of religions is simply unacceptable. It is right, and indeed necessary, for the good of men, that the non-Christian religions should hold to their own, at least until they find themselves in fact understood, translated, and included in the growing power of a religion which in achieving its own full potentiality, achieves theirs also.

* Ballad of the White Horse.

IS RELIGIOUS VARIETY TO PERSIST?

As we think of these varied excellences, the impression recurs that religions have their physiognomies and personal traits. Among persons there is no equivalence —no one can be substituted for any other: God created many individuals, each perfect and imperfect in a different place, instead of producing one solitary compendious embodiment of all human perfection. Are religions like persons in the respect that not all the possible virtues can be compressed into any one of them? And if so, is our original requirement that the world faith should be particular, like the abandoned ideal of a particular world state, somehow mistaken and impoverishing?

We are not asking the superfluous question whether all religious diversity should be abolished. No universal canopy of religion could cancel the need for the local functions of religion and its local histories. Sectarian differences also have their uses: a universal religion would be intolerable unless it allowed for the continuous birth (and reabsorption) of future varieties of experience and of thought. The only question is whether the distinctions which persist ought all to be held within the frame of a single concrete religion, especially those differences which now mark the individual geniuses of the great religious systems. Must they be conserved in any possible world faith? And if so, would the result be a unity? If Buddhism, for example, were to take up into itself the character of Christianity, would it still be Buddhism? If Christianity were to absorb into itself whatever marks the soul of Buddhism, would it still be Christianity? Or, as the several religions are clarified by one another, and with the growth of general enlightenment become alike in substance, is it any longer needful that there be a single name over all?

We have no need to anticipate what future course the process of uniting the religious mind of mankind will follow. But this residual question has at least a partial answer, and some of the factors which provide the answer are at hand. One of these factors is the nature, of the impulse which drives mankind towards unity mental and moral. This impulse is primarily religious, not cultural nor political. Or more precisely, the need for understanding among men, and the need for identity of religion are not two needs but one. The identity of the ultimate object of thought and value *is* the possibility of understanding.

And precisely because we do not want a world state, we do require a world morale; we can endure the absence of a world-administration just in so far as men of the most diverse racial and cultural stripe can retain confidence in one another, and so in the possibility of raising conflict out of the region of strife into the region of thought and justice. Without confidence on the part of the weaker peoples in the will to be just of the stronger, and without confidence of the stronger in the capacity to be just of the weaker, it is inconceivable that either should relinquish his advantage of strength or number in behalf of any communal effort for public righteousness. If the free adjustments of reason are ever to replace the adjustments of force and fraud, two conditions are necessary. First that this very heterogeneous mankind shall be able to discuss their issues, i.e. shall be able to think together, because they have in common science, logic, and the standard of right—they must have the same god. Second, that they shall come to *feel* together in regard to what is good and what constitutes human welfare—they must *worship* the same god. Of these two, the emotional unity is more important and far more difficult to realise.

Having the same god might conceivably be achieved under religions nominally different. The philosopher's god is the same being under whatever name. The diverse apparitions and images of God present varying and incommensurable qualities: but underneath all is the fundamental spirit of righteous and loving will. There is indeed one religion which is pre-eminently the religion of love; yet " 'Love one another' is probably a fundamental law of nature, a law as inexorable as the first law of thermodynamics."*

But to have the same god does not ensure the sameness of worship. Emotional unity does not come about by agreement of beliefs about the good. Just as in aesthetic matters understanding comes about by agreement on particular objects of art, so in moral matters it comes about by agreement on particular objects of esteem and reverence. For the deeper stages of emotional understanding men have need of a common

* Alexis Carrel, M.D.

and concrete symbol of regard and faith. And just because the racial variety of mankind provides so wide a gamut of emotional difference, and expresses itself so naturally in different and incomparable religious symbols, this need for a common symbol—not incompatible with the diverse symbols—*grows* as the arrival of a world culture calls for increasing co-operation across racial and temperamental lines.

The other factor of which I shall speak is an individual need, the need which arises from that deepening lostness of the soul in the expanding world which it is the direct function of religion to meet.

It is easy to speak of "world order"; it is not easy to realise the magnitude of the interests which are to be "ordered" still less can we estimate the cost of world order in terms of individual suffering and defeat. We are only beginning to realise how much anonymous sacrifice is to be called for, not alone of tangible goods but of reputes, courages, services, wise plans buried in futility, loves and patriotisms, rich local grandeurs and nobilities of character smudged away into nonentity, as the vast chaos grinds its insensate way towards becoming a moving system. The purity of one's passion for righteousness and for the spread of righteousness is no security against failure in this wild mill of history which no human mind is great enough to envisage, still less to direct.

If men are to keep their hearts, they must have some way of seeing the non-futility of the futile! They have to be assured that there is *another reckoning* in which what they have done and what they are has its effect, is known, comes to the centre. They need to know that what they have done to the least and in the least corner of the unsurveyable swirl of world-happening, they have done to the Highest.

But very probably they need the impossible! History must have a peculiar structure in order to realise such a condition. What structure? The Whole alive in every conscious part; the One somehow present in the interstices of happening, aware like some all-sensitive Karma-principle of every intent, every purpose there flashing into being, and linking it somewhere with its due effect. The ultimate transactions of history must be minutely careful of the absolute effectiveness of love and faith *there* in the world, among the particulars in which they intend to operate; the puny personal will at every point in immediate contact with an invisible, non-assertive omnipotent Tao—but a Tao who wills as if the whole infinite, irrelevant mass of detail in space and time were intended for and addressed to each individual soul alone! The logic of history in the last analysis a personal logic.

Surely a preposterous picture! The scientific view of the world lends it no *prima facie* support. As a set of physical events, the world has no focus in the individual self; the causal process flows through him and flows on; nothing terminates in him; no intentionality addresses itself to him; the blind events of an incalculable environment blindly impinge, penetrate, pass on.

The apparent structure of history changes at once when we recognise the magic wrought by consciousness: the qualities of the world are there *for the per-*

ceiving mind, and only for the perceiver—nothing so footless as to attribute colours to an unseeing Nature! The world has colour for the seer, it has sound for the hearer, odour and flavour for smell and taste. In terms of such qualities, the sunset and the foliage and the pageantry of the night skies exist for me and are as addressed to me, the perceiver. Yet not to me as an individual, for they expand themselves over all such as I am.

Is there a still deeper reason and magic hidden in the structure of events? Is it possible that the vast universe through some infinite multiplicity of focussing is, or can become, for each individual something personally addressed?

It is, I think, a unique element of Christianity that it declares this paradox to be the truth of things and sets this belief into its symbol. I know of no other religion which rises to this point of audacity, offering to every man, every forgotten atom, the possibility of fulfilling his will. It declares that history is in fact *personalised* in its invisible structure, in such wise that each life, especially then when it is most conscious of futility, may through its way achieve dignity and power.

As I study the foundation of the mind of our time, especially its underlying confidence, I am impressed by the degree to which it is actually using this conception of history even when it is consciously professing belief in a radically impersonal world-process. Faith in the significance of the particular event and of the individual person has become an almost subconscious factor in the western intuition of the world. What is the support of that faith? It is the omnipresent effect of an ancient personal achievement which through its silent pervasiveness has become all but anonymous. It was through the deeds of a carpenter of Nazareth that the overt formlessness of history seemed momentarily pushed aside like a drab curtain, disclosing a context in which space, time, number became unimportant, and every living thing stood vested in potential worth. This momentary perception, unprovable but commanding, remains to offset the increasing lostness of the individual in our modern world, even when its source is forgotten.

And as the voices of racial, national, organisational pride recede, the inescapable inheritance of these deeds will recur to conscious recognition.

I do not say "ascendancy"; for "recognition" is sufficient. No symbol can be an obligatory symbol. The figure of Christ can never serve the cause of world faith as the perquisite of a favoured group, still less as an escape from induced fears. "Accept this sign or perish" is an attitude which now incites rejection, because the spirit of man has become too much informed by Christianity. As a privilege, the Christ symbol "will draw all men"; as a threat never. But as the meaning of this symbol becomes purified of partisanship and folly, rejection becomes arbitrary, its temper will pass, and the perfect interpretation of the human heart will assume its due place. When "*In hoc signo*" ceases to be a battle cry, it will ascend as token of another conquest, the conquest of estrangement among the seekers of God.

"A VENTURE IN UNDERSTANDING"

THE following is a résumé of the results of a year of experience by Rev. C. Burnell Olds in Okayama, Japan, several years ago, in bringing together representatives of different faiths for conference on the common problems of religion. It is abbreviated from his account published under the above title :*

We are reminded by a recent magazine article that the world is on the way to mutual understanding, and that this understanding is leading us from intolerance to tolerance, and from tolerance to equality. This is true in the Orient also, even in religious circles, though none of us would flatter ourselves that we have arrived. Still we *are* on the way.

An effort that we are making in this direction here in Okayama is worthy of attention I believe, not so much for what it has accomplished as for the evidence that it gives that a new attitude is developing. It has grown out of the belief that we all, Christians, Buddhists, Shintoists, or whatever other faith, have much to learn from each other and much to contribute to each other. Also we feel that if as spiritual leaders we are to accomplish anything constructive for the good of society as a whole we ought first to get together as religionists and come to know each other sympathetically. We believe that as a result of such contacts our motives will be deepened and purified and our faith strengthened. We *are* brothers in a common quest, and the first step is to recognise it and disarm ourselves of our prejudices.

With the conviction that this could be done, I set out first, then, simply to get acquainted with some of the best representatives of the several religious sects that were operating in our city or its immediate vicinity. I called first on the leading priest of the Shin sect, visiting him in his temple, where we had a

* Reprinted with kind permission of Mr. Olds and of the *Missionary Herald*.

delightful conference together for two hours or more regarding the deeper spiritual values of our lives. We had not gone far in our talk together before it became evident to me that here, so far as I was concerned, was an unworked mine of spiritual possibilities, and so far as he was concerned, a readiness, yes, a hunger, for something more than he had yet got. Thinking there must be others like him also, I at length, with some hesitation, suggested the possibility and the desirability of our getting together, a few earnest spirits of us from the different sects of the several religions represented in the community, with the frank and avowed purpose of sharing with each other as friends the deepest spiritual experiences of our lives as they had come to us through our several religious faiths. The suggestion met with his instant approval, and thereupon we together formulated a plan and made out a list of those who might well be brought into such a group. They must be kindred spirits, not argumentative, not intrenched in prejudice, for all discussions must be on the plane of experience rather than of dogmatism or theory, and there must be no furtive effort at propaganda. Everyone must be honest with himself, not surrendering his faith or softening down his convictions, but outspoken and sincere, holding to what he believed to be the truth and ready to declare it, and yet maintaining a tolerant and open mind. Those were hard conditions to fulfil, so our men had to be chosen carefully. But we made out our list; one each from five of the leading Buddhist sects in Japan, since all happened to have representatives in Okayama—Shinshu, Shingon, Zen, Tendai, and Nichiren—and besides them, one pure Shintoist and three Christians of whom one is a well-known pastor and social worker, one a prominent layman, equally well-known and respected, and myself, an American missionary.

*   *   *   *   *

It was a full year since the venture described above was launched and the account written. Since then, with exception of August, we have met regularly every month, the group being entertained by each member in turn, with full evening meal served. The subjects discussed were varied in character, but were all vital. Here are some of them, in addition to those already mentioned: "Our Objective in Religion," two meetings; "The attitude that we should take toward Official Shinto," one meeting; "The Place of Rites and Symbols in Religion," two meetings, "Prayer as an attitude necessary to all Religion," one meeting; "Prayer as a personal experience," two meetings; "Superstition and Faith," two meetings.

*   *   *   *   *

And now what has come out of the year's experience? In the first place, the interest of the entire group has been maintained throughout the year. All are enthusiastic, all are for continuing, and all are jealous of the privilege of membership, desiring still to limit the group to a chosen few that the intimate nature of the conference may be maintained.

In the second place there is manifest throughout the group, as a result of the year's association, a depth of mutual understanding and goodwill, together with a breadth of sympathy and humility of spirit that was not there when we first came together.

Thirdly, it has opened up for me at least, unlimited avenues of communication with men of other religions. I have called on all the members of the group, and on scores of priests and leaders of their sects and other sects, and I have always found them cordially disposed, always ready to meet me halfway. In turn, several of them have called on me. I was asked at one time to give an extended Christian lecture to a group of young Shingon priests in one of the largest temples in the city and they were more than interested. I was invited also to the dedication of the new temple, the one referred to above, and though it was on Easter Sunday afternoon, my participation in it gave me a religious thrill that will not soon be forgotten. I can see now the shining face of the donor as he stood up there in the presence of the assembled crowd, and, in a few words choked with emotion, told them, in reply to their query as to why he had given the money, that Kannon Sama, the Goddess of Mercy had told him to do it and he couldn't help himself, I have also spoken at other temple meetings and rejoiced in the privilege.

And fourthly, it has driven us all away from our defences and out into the open field, where we are not afraid to challenge each other as to our views of life's supreme values.

Yes, it is a venture, and we don't yet know what will come of it, even after a year's trial of it. Perhaps not much. But it is our conviction that the approach we are making to each other is worth while, and the attitude that is thus called forth, even within this narrow circle, may go out to influence other lives, and whole areas of lives, even as a stone dropped into a stagnant pool starts circles that go on widening ever.

One thing seems to me to be true. If we are ever to reach Buddhists and others like them and hope to develop in them a right attitude of mind toward the larger truth of religion, we must have the same attitude of mind ourselves and meet them as equals. Then we can give our best and they can give theirs, and the result will be as salutary for us as for them. But if we assume the attitude taken by one prominent missionary of long experience in the Orient, that we have after all, nothing to learn from other cultures or faiths, then we may expect to find the way not only closed to a far-reaching influence among them, but may experience a gradual dwarfing of our own spiritual natures that will end in spiritual atrophy and death.

And of one other thing I am also convinced, and that is that to have a mind and heart open to the winds of heaven, to receive the inspiration that may be breathed by the Spirit through the experiences of men of faiths differing from my own, may result in making me less of a propagandist within the limits of my sect, but more of a Christian whose one aim is the establishment of the Kingdom of God through the operation of the spirit of love and goodwill which is the central motive in the experience of Jesus Christ. Therefore, let no one think that my loyalty to him and to his spirit has diminished. Rather it has been vitalised, thanks to my excursions into the experiences of men of faiths other than my own.

A STATEMENT OF THE CONTENT
OF CHRISTIANITY*

IN respect to its theology and ethics, Christianity has many doctrines in common with other religions, yet no other religion has the same group of doctrines. It would be difficult to point out any one general principle which could surely be found nowhere else. But there is no need—it is a humiliating mistake —for Christianity to contest priority or uniqueness in regard to these general ideas. There is no property here: what is true belongs, in its nature, to the human mind everywhere.

From this treasury of thought, however, Christianity proffers a selection which is unique. The principle of selection is its own peculiar character: its individuality lies in the way in which it assembles and proportions these truths, and lends to them clarity, certainty, exemplification, and therefore power. Its features, like the features of a person, are unmistakably its own.

* The following statement is based on a draft made in the Spring and Summer of 1932, in the course of my work as Chairman of the Commission of Appraisal appointed by the Laymen's Foreign Missionary Inquiry. The original draft was submitted to the Commission for discussion. In its present form it constitutes the major part of chapter three of the report of this Commission, "Rethinking Missions." As a matter of course, it was necessary to indicate the range of difference which obtains among Protestants in their views of the nature of Jesus. In this present printing, I have defined in a footnote my own position within this range, as I naturally did not define it in the Report. It will be observed that this device of stating at a crucial point the actual divergence of opinion avoided the three besetting evils of all such corporate statements, namely, (1) saying nothing, (2) compromising somebody or everybody, (3) minority reports. The statement, in which all fifteen members of the commission concurred, remains in my judgment valid, though there are many things which I would like to say about Christianity, and am planning to say in an early writing, for which there was here no scope.

It is of the essence of Christianity that its central teachings are simple.

It was one aspect of the genius of Jesus that amid a rich store of earlier codes and doctrines he discerned what was essential and brought it to brief and forcible expression. The essence of the law he states in the two great commandments; the essence of right conduct in the Golden Rule; the essence of prayer in the Lord's Prayer; the essence of theology in the picture of God as Father; the essence of the social ideal in the vision of the Kingdom of Heaven among men.

Christianity is not an easy teaching; but the qualifications for grasping it, the ear to hear and the will to obey, are primarily moral and were first achieved by untutored fishermen; whereas its difficulties are said to be chiefly for those who, ruled by their possessions or entangled in affairs or befogged by seeming wisdom, find it hard to return to the direct intuitions of childhood.

If, then, the Orient is anywhere unresponsive to our complex theologies (and here we think especially of China), the implication may be not that the Orient is dull towards Christianity, but that these complexities are too little Christian, too much the artefacts of our western brains.

The simplicity of Christianity is a part of its uniqueness.

It is evident that much of the spiritual value of Christianity in the Orient is its power of release from the intricacies which have grown up within the great polytheistic systems. There is a conservative impulse in religion which has its own justification, but which, in retaining primitive practices and ideas, frequently incongruous with one another, accumulates confusion by its very loyalties. This is especially true of Hinduism. The presence of even a small Christian community, holding to its few essentials of religion, ensures that these same essentials will do a persistent work of sifting within these conglomerate traditions of Asia.

The Christianity which thus works silently, by the inherent power of a valid focus, within these ancient bodies presupposes a Christian group which maintains its own distinctness. When simplicity is merged with complexity, simplicity is lost. There must be a group of believers who can illustrate the "pure instance" of an Oriental Christianity.

And further, only a religion whose first principles are capable of the simplest formulation can become a religion for the modern man, whether in the Orient or elsewhere. The religion which assumes too much knowledge of the supernatural realm, its system of heavens and hells, or its inner mechanisms of eternal justice, can no longer be a living issue.

But the uniqueness of Christianity does not consist solely in its interpretation of religious truth. It consists also, perhaps chiefly, in those things which make religion different from all philosophy—its symbolism, its observances, its historical fellowship, and especially the personal figure to whom it points not alone as founder and teacher, but as its highest expression of the religious life. In these matters Christianity is necessarily unique.

In them it is also rich. The great simplicity of its doctrine is not inconsistent with wealth in symbol, imagery and story. Religion has to speak to the emotions and the will, not to the intellect alone. Further, the historical and imaginative elements of religion are not mere illustrations or adornments of faith; they are parts of its meaning. When religious truth is drained off into a set of propositions divorced from their emotional setting, it is somewhat less than true. The narratives and parables of the Gospel, unique in the sacred literature of the world, have probably influenced the lives of men far more than the exacter formulations of faith.

In general, our Protestant Churches, as compared with Roman Catholic and Buddhist, have made too little of the concrete and poetic elements of religion, conveyed through all the forms of art, through local setting and ritual expression. To the Oriental this lack is an impediment; for the symbolic and personal expression of religion is his native channel for appreciating it.

Symbols without explanations run to theological mummery; explanations without symbols run to philosophical dry bones.

Into the person of Jesus, as the central symbol as well as the central historic reality of their faith, Christians are prone to compress its entire meaning. Hence it has been customary for Christian bodies in announcing their message to mankind to say compactly, "Our message is Jesus Christ."

This language, full of meaning as it is for those who already know what Jesus stands for, is of course full of mystery for those who do not. To the average Oriental, without further explanation, it could mean nothing. Even to many a contemporary in the West, unused to the language of the Churches, it means little more than a current phrase marking loyalty to a tradition somewhat undefined in his thought. In our own effort to present the message of Christianity, we desire to use the privilege of laymen in avoiding as far as possible the language of the unexplained symbol. We believe it to be one of the necessities of the present hour that Christianity should be able to make more immediate connection with common experience and thought. Especially in addressing the Orient it is imperative that we present our faith in terms which those wholly unfamiliar with the history of Christian doctrine can understand.*

To a world of men preoccupied with the struggle for living amid the actualities of physical facts and laws and of social relations Christianity, with other religions, declares that the most real of all realities, the most momentous for human concern, is the unseen spirit within and beyond these visible things, God.

For Christianity, God is not far off; but in all our actions we are dealing with him whether we know it or not; in plowing,

---

* In our statement we shall dwell little on those contrasts between Christianity and other religions which scholars have been at so much pains to define. The growth within these religions, the new knowledge of their history, the arrival of new sects within them, make such contrasts always insecure. We shall rather attempt to give a positive account of the way in which Christianity meets the issues which Oriental religions raise, with incidental reference to broad diverging tendencies. It is not necessary that Christianity should announce, define and insist on superiorities at this point and that; it is necessary that it be certain of what it lives by, and live by it.

sowing, reaping; in the work of home, shop, office, in effort and rest, in success and failure, God is present, imperceptible, forceless, all powerful. He is an undiscerned strength to those who serve their fellow men. Those who ignore him fail of truth and build on what is perishable.

Though God is everywhere present, Christianity holds that God is also One; so that in the world there is one purpose and one divine power with whom we have to deal—not many.

Christianity is prepared with the polytheistic faiths to see God in varied aspects. Since he is present in all events, the sensitive soul, whether seer or poet or peasant, may perceive him at many turns and in many guises; the richness of life is enhanced by these numerous meetings. Those are the poor, for whom the shell of finite appearance never breaks.

But in all these myriad discernings the being of God is not dispersed, nor his character varied. If there is a God in the pain or in the terror of the world, it is the same God as appears in its beauty; this is the only hope for the ultimate conquest of evil. Nor are these events in which God appears removed from the realm of natural law; to the unity of nature corresponds the unity of the divine will. It is only through this unity that the sciences are freed for their full work, unhampered by threatened intrusions from the supernatural.

Though the world is a world of law, the supreme law of the world is not physical but moral. The reality of men and of societies consists not in wealth and force but in their inner moral quality; it is this which governs their destiny. This truth is common to the great religions.

For Christianity, this means that God is a self, not an impersonal principle of moral order. With Buddhism, Christianity would assert that at the heart of all happening in the universe there is a rigorous law of moral consequence, holding over from the visible to the invisible reaches of destiny. With Buddhism also, this law of retribution is subject to a higher principle, admitting release. For Christianity this higher principle is a personal love, actively seeking to win the human soul to a new relationship with itself, and therewith to righteousness and peace.

For Christianity, the truth that God is holy as well as loving implies that he is not capricious, nor vengeful in his justice, nor moved by desire to which men can minister except by inward fidelity and love. He is therefore not to be moved by gifts and sacrifices, nor in need of conciliation: he can be worshipped only by pure and sincere hearts.

Christianity does not disapprove of nor dispense with visible symbols to aid the worshipper in the direction of his mind. But, as we conceive it, it rejects the identification of any of these material objects with deity. It is opposed to the belief that any such object or place or personal relic can be a source of divine or miraculous power.

Nevertheless, Christianity believes in the real presence of God in personal life and teaches that the highest privilege of religion is a direct experience of companionship with God and union with his will.

In this experience, the Christian finds what in the Orient is often sought as "realisation." But Christianity teaches that this union with God is a result, not of a special and difficult technique, nor of asceticism and the abandonment of human ties; but rather of a pure devotion to God's will which is at the same time and inseparably a love for the divine possibilities in other human beings, one's brothers.

Hence religion cannot be realised by solitary self-discipline alone, but by active loyalty to some person or cause in which the welfare of men is involved. God's Kingdom, to the Christian, is to be established among men; hence he is never free to give over the course of human affairs to forces of evil or disorder.

On the other hand, the realisation of human welfare requires the deepening of the self by reflection, meditation and self-mastery. Hence practical religion tends to be an alternate or double process of withdrawal from the world and immersion in the world of prayer and social activity.

The proportions of these two phases will vary widely with individual need. There are persons who may well give themselves very largely to the life of meditation, if only its results come eventually to the common good. There may be others chiefly given to "service," if only that activity reverts to its moment of the realisation of meaning.

If Hindu, Buddhist, or Taoist tend to exalt the ideal of the secluded and ascetic life to the detriment of the realization of God in human affairs, the practical spirit of the age may in reaction tend to identify religion with social performance. It must be emphasised that activity runs shallow, loses zest, meaning, and ultimately effect; and social efforts lose their power to cohere; unless they return from time to time to recruit the springs of the will in communion with the Great Will.

Christianity refers its conception of God, of man, and of religion to the teachings and life of Jesus.

It believes that in the course of history, the insistent problems of religion came to Jesus with peculiar clarity and force, and that he gave answers to them which, because of their simple and essential nature, may be taken as final. Further, he exemplified his own teaching in life and death, and affords to all men who come to know him the most transparent and accessible example of a life lived greatly through immediate union with God. Because this career was given wholly to manifesting the meaning of religion, and was carried through under the severest tests, it stands as a unique support to all who subsequently desire to carry out the same venture. After him, they can never be alone, whatever their hazards. He becomes in spirit their companion and master.

To many Christians, the life of religion becomes a life of actual fellowship with Jesus conceived as a living spirit, the Christ; and through union with him they are united with one another in the Church, the body of his followers. Christians differ in the metaphysical meaning to be assigned to this person and to this experience of union. To many of them the Christ fuses with the conception of God; and Jesus is called in a unique sense the "Son of God" or the "Incarnation of God." These doctrines may mean a profound spiritual union of the will of Jesus with the will of God;* for others, a more literal identity, attested by miracle in his birth, deeds, death, and resurrection. It is not our function to limit the range of these differences of conception, but rather to draw attention to the fact that they exist, and that beneath them are underlying agreements, belonging to the essence of Christianity, as a positive and historical religion.

Since Christianity unites the love of God with the love of men, its theology at once flows out into a conception of rightful human relationships.

The great religions agree that it is the office of religion in human affairs to make prevalent the spirit of sympathy and love. To some of them, this spirit operates in a realm of illusion where in the end no private interest matters, and no private self is real. Compassion and kindness are chiefly disciplines for destroying in oneself the root of selfishness, thus overcoming the moral illusion of separate selfhood.

To the Christian also, selfishness is the enemy. But the love of men which destroys its root is directed to real issues. For it holds that each individual soul matters in the sight of God, and that those who love men are but perceiving their true and absolute worth. The idea of the immortality of the soul is the measure of the soul's intrinsic dignity. This conception of the worth of the individual person becomes in personal life the final basis for self-respect and for inescapable responsibility; in social life it builds the structure of rights and also of duties.

For Christianity, the spirit of love is the guiding principle in meeting all specific ethical problems.

* This is my own position.

With the instinctive life and its perversities—with greed, lust, anger, pride—the teachings of Jesus deal expressly and poignantly. The Sermon on the Mount translocates the issues of right and wrong from the outward act to the inner motive. Adultery is identified with lust. Property, however lawfully owned, is a danger to the soul: its health demands a moral freedom from all possessions, an absence of anxiety for the morrow. The problems of injury and wrath are not solved by the legalities of justice: the enemy is to be loved, and to the smiter one must turn the other cheek. Epoch-making dicta for the dispositions of the heart; their clear radicalism flows from an unerring sense of what things are first in the values of life.

These same sayings become the basis for an inward renewal of social life. They do not contain specific solutions for the social problems set by pugnacity, property, and sex. There is nothing in their authority to spare Christians who would apply them the effort of thought.

In the practices of Christendom which stand in glaring contrast to the words of the Sermon on the Mount, there is ground for humiliation. Our message to the Orient must be accompanied by our confession: the standards we profess are not the positions we have attained. In many ways Christianity is farther beyond the behaviour of the Christian world than it is beyond the behaviour of portions of the Orient.

At the same time it should be said that our departures from the literal injunctions of this Sermon are not wholly matters of bad conscience: those words do not define, and were not intended to define, our social ideals. "Take no thought" cannot be used as a maxim for the economic life of man in the society of to-day. "Turn the other cheek" is not a solution for the problems of legal and political justice. The spirit of love alone does not meet the immediate problems set by national aggression or by competition. Side by side with the great sayings of Jesus which declare the dangers of passionate impulse, and the primary importance of "the Kingdom of God, and its righteousness," there are others which declare the moral value of an abundant life, implying the full development of human nature: the Sermon on the Mount is not the whole of his teaching. There must be a right use of sex, of pugnacity, of wealth. These right uses are, for our time, problems incompletely solved. They are problems for all the great religions, especially for those which like Christianity, Buddhism, the Vedanta, see the necessity for an inner renunciation and detachment before human desires may safely be given freedom to weave their fabrics in the world of experience.

While these problems are being worked out, the spirit of their solution is present. Through Jesus and through such wills as his, God works throughout human history bringing men towards unity in a love which is universal in its sweep.

This spirit establishes and makes sacred the family tie. It extends beyond the family to the nation and to other social groups, as far as they are ready to admit love and justice as elements of control. It extends to the most difficult international and interracial adjustments, as humanity learns what righteousness requires in the conduct of world affairs.

Christianity regards no human grouping as sacred in itself: none can command absolute loyalty. The stability of them all— family, economic order, nation—is conditional upon the loyalty of each member to something beyond the group itself, the spirit of love and justice, which is God. In this sense, it is the law of history that men and groups must lose their lives in order to save them.

INDEX